Why Do They Call It a Birdie?

1,001 Fascinating Facts about Golf

Frank Coffey

CITADEL PRESS
Kensington Publishing Corp.
www.kensingtonbooks.com

CITADEL PRESS books are published by

Kensington Publishing Corp.
850 Third Avenue
New York, NY 10022

All Kensington titles, imprints, and distributed lines are available at special quantity discounts for bulk purchases for sales promotions, premiums, fund raising, educational, or institutional use. Special book excerpts or customized printings can also be created to fit specific needs. For details, write or phone the office of the Kensington special sales manager: Kensington Publishing Corp., 850 Third Avenue, New York, NY 10022, attn: Special Sales Department, phone 1-800-221-2647.

First printing 1998

10 9 8 7 6 5 4 3 2

Printed in the United States of America

Library of Congress Cataloging-in-Publication Data

Coffey, Frank
    Why do they call it a birdie? : 1,001 fascinating facts about golf
  / Frank Coffey.
     p. cm.
    ISBN 1-55972-429-3
    1. Golf—Miscellanea. 2. Golfers—Rating of. 3. Golf—History.
  I. Title.
  GV965.C595   1997
  796.352—dc21   97-21506
                                           CIP

Contents

Preface

"If the sun is up, why aren't you playing golf?"
—Lee Trevino

"One of the most fascinating things about golf is how it reflects the cycle of life. No matter what you shoot, the next day you have to go back to the first tee and begin all over again and make yourself into something."
—Peter Jacobsen

"I've always dreamed of coming up 18 and winning."
—Tiger Woods

All of life is cyclical and, as I write this, the game of golf is at the top of the cycle. The reason is pretty simple: Tiger Woods. At twenty-one, he is the most exciting and best player the game has seen since young Jack Nicklaus ("Fat Jack" back then) emerged a star some thirty years ago. He may be the best ever, according to no less an authority than the aforementioned Nicklaus.

When the aptly nicknamed Tiger (real name, Eldrick) won the '97 Masters by 12 strokes—the widest margin of victory in the tournament's 63 years—with the lowest score, 270, the world of golf was changed forever. Rarely does one see the old guard replaced by the new so dramatically. In four astonishingly brilliant days Tiger crowned himself King, promising a long and fruitful reign for himself and all his subjects. A multiracial kid from the public courses of Los Angeles had just delivered the greatest performance ever seen in a golf major. We, the world, had witnessed history made before our eyes and knew instantly that it was good and pure and breathtakingly revolutionary.

From a writer's point of view, this is also a wonderful time to be publishing a golf book, for golf is more than a game. It's a way of life and a culture. It has its own rules, code of behavior, courses, equipment, fashions, history, anecdotes, jargon, and its own special kind of humor. It is a complex world that is also simple. It takes time to understand, but what one puts into the game, one can also take out. That is, the game ultimately is rewarding.

This book will familiarize you with fun facts related to all of the above elements of golf. You could call it an entertainment of facts. Consider it to be, not an introduction to how to play golf, but a starter kit for understanding all that surrounds the game. Golf today is energized and renewed—everything old is new again. The future is now.

More than 50 million golfers are on the planet today. If you're not one of them, or if you're a recent convert, *Why Do They Call It a Birdie?* will help your growth curve. If you're already a player (or fan or zealot) this book will help remind you why.

Most of all, golf is a game to be enjoyed. On a blue-sky day replete with puffy white clouds, strolling down a fairway with golf clubs and friends is a little bit of heaven on earth. The goal of *Why Do They Call It a Birdie?* is to help you strollers appreciate the walk.

Golf in the United States

Here's some basic information on golf and golfers in the United States. Feel free, while reveling at your favorite nineteenth-hole emporium, to trot out these figures as if you've known them all your life.

- There are 25 million golfers in the United States today. Of this number, approximately 50 percent play eight or more rounds a year.
- 5.5 million "avid golfers" play twenty-five or more rounds per year.
- There are 15,390 golf courses in the United States. Of these, 69 percent are open to the public.
- 490 million rounds of golf are played in the United States each year.
- Golfers buy $15 billion worth of golf merchandise and equipment yearly.
- Each year, 2 million people play golf for the first time. Nearly 40 percent of them are women.
- Women make up 21.5 percent of the golfing population.
- 3.5 million senior citizens (sixty and older) play golf.

Why Do They Call It a Birdie?

1

Quiz: What's Your Golfing I.Q.?

Golf is a puzzle without an answer.
—GARY PLAYER

Before proceeding, let's see just how much you know about the game of golf—history, terminology, rules, etiquette. There are fifty questions, some simple, some obscure—two points for each. Because you bought this book, I'm going to be merciful and assign a generous rating system: If you get half right, you pass—that is to say, you're not a golf idiot. (The three bonus questions will help you get over the hump.)

Answers are on p. 8.

Questions

1. Where was the modern game of golf invented?

2. What tournaments are known as the majors?

3. How many clubs is a player allowed for tournament play by the United States Golf Association (USGA)?

4. What does the word *lie* mean?

5. Who said, "Golf is a good walk spoiled"?

6. What golfer is famous for incessant chattering on the links?

7. Who is the Golden Bear?

8. Name four golfers who won all four majors.

9. What's an *address* in golf?

10. True or false? A caddie does nothing but carry a golfer's clubs.

11. What is the one element in nature that can officially stop a golf game?

12. What famous golfer was involved in a collision with a bus but returned successfully to golf?

13. What is the Walker Cup?

14. Are the clubfaces of woods flat, or rounded from top to bottom?

15. Name three golfers of Hispanic ancestry.

16. What great golfer is famous for his slashing stroke?

17. What are the two main types of putters?

18. Who was the first foreign golfer to win the Masters?

19. What is an "albatross"?

20. Name the three Great Triumvirates.

21. What was Babe Didrikson Zaharias's real first name?

22. Does "bumping the ball" refer to an accidental act or one done on purpose?

23. Who won the most British Opens and what golfing technique is named after him?

24. Who was the author of *The Little Black Book*?

25. What are the "yips"?

26. Who was the father of American golf?

27. What is the difference between the "cup" and the "hole"?

28. What is "gutta-percha"?

29. What famous golfer was hit by lightning?

30. True or false? You're expected to replace your divots on a golf course.

31. Who was the first golfer inducted into the Ladies' Professional Golf Association (LPGA) Hall of Fame?

32. Is a game of golf nine or eighteen holes long?

33. What is Gene Sarazen's real last name?

34. The numbers 382 and 384, often seen on golf balls, refer to what?

35. What do Pete Dye, Robert Trent Jones Jr., and Jack Nicklaus all have in common?

36. What is Arnie's Army and who is the General?

37. Which is more important during the swing—to keep your head down or to keep it still?

38. Who is the Great White Shark?

39. What does *plus fours* refer to in golf?

40. True or false? The term *bogey* is derived from *bogey man*.

41. What's a "Texas wedge"?

42. What does "pulling the pin" refer to?

43. What's the difference between "par" and "even par"?

44. What twelve-year-old golfer won the New Mexico Amateur in 1969?

45. True or false? A club referred to as a "wood" may be made of metal.

46. What does a *rabbit* refer to in golf?

47. On which hand is the golfing glove worn?

48. What color jacket is awarded to the winner of the Masters?

49. What club is a beginner generally advised to tee off with?

50. What three players were golf's first millionaires?

Bonus question 1   What else besides playing golf is Jack Nicklaus known for?

Bonus question 2   What golfer underwent a newsworthy change of hairstyle?

Bonus question 3   What golfer dominated the 1943 PGA, the 1943–45 Masters, the 1942–45 U.S. Opens, and the 1940–45 British Opens?

Tiger Woods

1. Scotland.
2. The British Open, the U.S. Open, the Masters, and the PGA Championship.
3. 14.
4. The spot where the ball is sitting.
5. Mark Twain.
6. Lee Trevino.
7. Jack Nicklaus.
8. Gene Sarazen, Ben Hogan, Gary Player, and Jack Nicklaus.
9. The moment when a player positions his body and club in readiness to play a shot.
10. False—a caddie also offers advice on club selection and play strategy.
11. Lightning.
12. Ben Hogan.
13. An amateur team match involving Britain, Ireland, and the United States.
14. Rounded.
15. Lee Trevino, Chi Chi Rodriguez, and Nancy Lopez.
16. Arnold Palmer.
17. Center-shafted and heel-shafted.
18. South African Gary Player in 1961.
19. A double eagle.
20. The first Great Triumvirate in golf was James Braid, John Taylor, and Harry Vardon, who dominated the game at the turn of the century. The second Great Triumvirate was Ben Hogan, Byron Nelson, and Sam Snead, who dominated in the 1940s and early 1950s. The third Great Triumvirate

was Arnold Palmer, Gary Player, and Jack Nicklaus of the 1960s and 1970s.

21. Mildred.
22. Both—and either way, it's cheating unless you score it properly.
23. Harry Vardon, six times; he popularized a technique known as the Vardon grip.
24. Byron Nelson.
25. Nervousness before a shot, usually referring to a twitching of the hands on a putt.
26. John Reid.
27. Nothing—both terms refer to what you're aiming for.
28. A material similar to rubber tapped from various species of tropical trees, once used to make golf balls.
29. Lee Trevino.
30. True.
31. Patty Berg.
32. Either.
33. Saraceni.
34. The number of dimples on the ball surface.
35. They're all designers of golf courses.
36. Arnold Palmer's fans; they like to call him "General."
37. It's more important to keep your head still so as not to alter the swing.
38. Greg Norman.
39. Knickers, once popular in golf fashion—*plus fours* refers to the four inches added to shorts to make them extend over the knee.
40. True.
41. A Texas wedge refers to a putter used from off the green.

42. Removing the flagstick from the hole for putting.
43. No difference.
44. Nancy Lopez.
45. True.
46. A novice golfer.
47. The left hand (if right-handed).
48. Green.
49. A 3-wood.
50. Arnold Palmer, Jack Nicklaus, and Gary Player.

Bonus 1 Designing golf courses.

Bonus 2 Jack Nicklaus—from crewcut to longish.

Bonus 3 Trick question, the answer is "none"—no tournaments were played in the years listed because of World War II.

2

An Overview of Golf History

There are two distinct kinds of golf—just plain golf and tournament golf. Golf—the plain variety—is the most delightful of games, an enjoyable companionable pastime; tournament golf is thrilling, heartbreaking, terribly hard work—a lot of fun when you are young with nothing much on your mind, but fiercely punishing in the end.

—BOBBY JONES

The traditions of the game are rich with memories of dramatic triumphs as well as heartbreaking failures. The best players fail the most because they are in the hunt all the time. You learn to handle it—accept it or you don't survive.

—DEANE BEMAN

The Men's Game

Although games bearing a similarity to golf extend as far back as the Roman Empire, the game that is recognizable to us as "golf" originated in Scotland in the early fifteenth century. The idea was to use a club to hit a small ball into a small hole.

A good notion. Golf became a national obsession that worried King James II of Scotland and the king's parliament. Scotland was at war with England, and it was feared that the game was distracting the populace too much from the practice of archery. Swinging a club might come in handy, but archery was the method by which the kingdom was defended. In any case, in 1457 it was announced in an act of the Scottish Parliament that "Fute-ball and Golfe be utterly cryed down." This was the first recorded reference to *golfe,* a word derived from the German word *kolbe* and Dutch *kolfe,* meaning "club."

King James IV was originally an adamant foe of golf, who in 1491, established a law against it. Playing was punishable by both fine and imprisonment. He later became a fan and, at the very end of the fifteenth century, ordered a set of "golf clubbis and ballis" for himself. In the sixteenth century, Mary Queen of Scots (Mary Stuart), his granddaughter, was an avid golfer and took the game to France when she ascended to the French throne through marriage. James VI of Scotland, who, as James I, was king of England in the early seventeenth century, and his son, Charles I, helped popularize the game there.

In the eighteenth century, two major golf organizations emerged: the Honourable Company of Edinburgh Golfers and the Society of St. Andrews, later called the Royal and Ancient Golf Club of St. Andrews. The latter became the established authority on the Rules of Golf and the governing body for golf in Britain.

Jack Nicklaus

In the United States organized golf dates from 1888, when the St. Andrews Golf Club was founded at Yonkers, New York, by a Scotsman, John Reid. Reid is known as the father of American golf.

From its beginning until the late 1890s, golf, though a popular sport, remained a game for amateurs. The United States Golfing Association (USGA) was founded in 1894. The first official amateur champion, Charles Blair MacDonald, was selected in 1895. Prior to the 1890s, a "professional golfing person" was merely one who gave lessons to amateurs. In the final decade of the nineteenth century, the British golfers—Harry Vardon, James Braid, and J. H. Taylor—the Great Triumvirate—became the first true "professional" golfers, earning their living by playing the sport competitively.

The first American hero of golf was twenty-year-old Francis Ouimet, who beat Harry Vardon and Ted Ray at the historic tournament of 1913 at the Country Club in Brookline, Massachusetts.

Year by year golf's popularity increased. By the 1920s, golf had become an affordable game for the common man. In that decade, too, golf had its first true "colorful" character: Walter Hagen, a good-humored, swaggering, larger-than-life American who won the 1922 British Open. Hagen epitomized the Roaring Twenties in the realm of golf with a showmanship that was very important to his image.

In 1930 Bobby Jones won the U.S. and British Opens and the U.S. and British Amateur championships—a feat referred to as the Grand Slam. New York City gave him a ticker-tape parade. With that accomplishment behind him, Jones retired from golf at the age of twenty-eight. Jones, a crowd favorite, was a purist—a man who played the game for the love of it rather than for a payoff. It's no exaggeration to state that Bobby Jones is the celestial reference point in international golf history.

In the 1930s, the majors—the U.S. Open, the British Open, the Masters, and the PGA (Professional Golfers Association) Championship—assumed their importance in tournament play and galvanized the sporting public. Yet the Great Depression meant the closing down of many small courses. Golf, for a time, became a game for professionals.

A dominant pre–World War II player was Gene Sarazen, "the Squire." In 1922 he won both the U.S. Open and the PGA. The one weakness in his game was getting out of sand traps. As a remedy, Sarazen took flying lessons from Howard Hughes to learn the aerodynamic principle of "lift" with the idea of applying it to golf. Sarazen refurbished his sand irons (niblicks) with solder. The result: His sand game improved, and in 1932 he won the U.S. Open and the British Open. Only Bobby Jones before him had won both titles in the same year. During the 1935 Masters, using a 4-wood, Sarazen went down in history with an incredible double-eagle on the 5-par fifteenth hole.

Bobby Jones reemerged in the 1930s as a golf course designer. With investor Clifford Roberts, he attempted to create the perfect golf course. They located 365 acres in Augusta, Georgia. "I knew the instant I saw it that I had found my dream course," Jones said. By 1935 the Augusta was established as an important tournament.

Byron Nelson was a superb golf technician of the late 1930s and the 1940s. In 1945 he won eighteen tournaments—eleven in a row. The fact that he had been rejected from military service and that many of his competitors were occupied with wartime activities may have enabled him to dominate the game.

Immediately after World War II, two of Nelson's foremost competitors, Sam Snead and Ben Hogan, returned to the links. Sam Snead, a handsome Texan full of homespun humor, became a favorite of the press. He was reported by many to have the "sweetest swing" they'd ever seen. Although he was a golfing superstar, Snead never won the U.S. Open. Ben Hogan was also a highly respected golfer. Far from a natural, he put himself through thousands of hours of rigorous practice. In 1949 he was involved in a road accident that left his body weakened, but he trained hard to return to the game and lost little. Hogan, Nelson, and Snead were golf's second Great Triumvirate.

In the late 1950s, Arnold Palmer dominated the golf scene and became firmly entrenched as the darling of the golf world. He was an aggressive daredevil on the links, trying shots few others would.

In the 1960s Palmer had to share the spotlight with two other greats—Jack Nicklaus and Gary Player. Together they became known as the Big Three or the third Great Triumvirate. From 1960 to 1967, they won half of the major championships between them. Initially Nicklaus had difficulty in gaining favor with the public despite his obvious abilities. Because he was a heavyset, awkward-looking kid, not as appealing as the lean and well-dressed Palmer, Nicklaus was viewed as an upstart. Yet the kid could play, and in time began to win over both spectators and the media. He lost weight and let his hair grow and graduated from being known as Fat Jack to being called the Golden Bear. Although Player never matched the consistency of Palmer and Nicklaus, he won all four majors and more than one hundred tournament victories.

In the late 1960s, the Big Three were joined by another golf superstar, Lee Trevino. Born in Mexico and affectionately known as Super Mex, Trevino built a reputation as a brilliant and colorful player. A chronic chatterbox on the links and a practical joker, he became a crowd favorite. At the 1971 Open, he tossed a rubber snake to Jack Nicklaus.

Tom Watson, a gifted player and top money-maker, dominated the game in the 1970s and early 1980s. Between 1975 and 1983, he won five British Opens. Often involved in dramatic golf duels with Jack Nicklaus, Watson eventually proved to be his successor.

In recent golf history, exciting players have included Johnny Miller, Seve Ballesteros, Greg Norman, Ben Crenshaw, and Nick Faldo.

In the mid-1990s, Tiger Woods, a young man of African-American and Asian ancestry, has emerged as a superstar, bringing new attention to the game of golf.

Paganica (the game of countryman) was a Roman game played with bent clubs and a ball made of feathers; *Chole* was a similar Flemish game; *jeu de mail*, a French version; and *kolven*, a Dutch game. It was the Scots, though, who developed the game we know today as golf.

In the early years of the Ladies Professional Golf Association (the LPGA—which began as the WPGA in 1946 and became the LPGA in 1949), Babe Didrikson Zaharias, Betty Jameson, Betsy Rawls, Louise Suggs, and Patty Berg dominated women's golf.

In the 1932 Olympics, Babe Didrikson Zaharias was a gold-medal winner as a sprinter. She was also a talented baseball player. When she finally turned to golf, she won seventeen consecutive tournaments between 1946 and 1947. From 1948 to 1953, she captured another twenty-four tournaments. In 1953 she was out of the game, battling against breast cancer. After returning to golf in 1954 and winning her third Women's Open, she told the crowds of spectators, "I said, 'Please, God, let me play again,' and He answered my prayer." In 1956, she succumbed to her illness, dying a legend at the age of forty-two.

In the 1960s Mickey Wright and Kathy Whitworth were the "big two" in women's golf. More recently, Pat Bradley, JoAnne Carner, and Nancy Lopez have dominated the game.

Lopez emerged in 1978 with nine tournament wins, five of them in a row. She was voted both the LPGA Rookie of the Year and Player of the Year. She has been a role model to women golfers and an inspirational athlete comparable to Babe Didrikson Zaharias.

Mary, Queen of Scots, loved golf. In 1567, just three days after her husband's death, she was seen playing a hole. The good Mary knew that husbands are temporary, golf is forever.

1457 In an act of the Scottish Parliament, King James II bans golf because it competes with archery practice.

1491 King James IV creates a more severe law against golf: Those caught playing will be fined and imprisoned.

1744 The Honourable Company of Edinburgh Golfers, the first golf association, is founded.

1754 The Society of St. Andrews (later called the Royal and Ancient Golf Club of St. Andrews), the governing body of golf in Britain, is founded.

1848 A new material resembling rubber is used in the making of golf balls—gutta-percha.

1860 The inaugural British Open is held.

1888 The St. Andrews Club of Yonkers is founded by John Reid, a Scotsman.

1893 Charles Blair MacDonald builds the first eighteen-hole golf course in the United States, at the Chicago Golf Club.

1894 The Amateur Golf Association—later the United States Golfing Association (USGA)—is founded.

1895 The USGA holds the first Men's Open, Men's Amateur, and Women's Amateur events.

1913 At the U.S. Open (held at the Country Club at Brookline, Massachusetts), Harry Vardon and Ted Ray (both British champions) are beaten by Francis Ouimet, a twenty-year-old American amateur.

1916 The Professional Golfers Association (PGA) of America is organized and the inaugural PGA Championship held.

1924–27 Walter Hagen wins four consecutive PGA titles—a still unbroken record.

1922 The first Walker Cup Match is won by the U.S. team.

1924 The USGA legalizes the steel-shafted putter.

1927 The first Ryder Cup Match is won by the U.S. team.

1929 The Royal and Ancient Golf Club of St. Andrews legalizes the use of steel shafts in tournament play in Britain.

1930 Bobby Jones wins the "Grand Slam"—the U.S. and British Opens and the U.S. and British Amateurs.

1932 The first Curtis Cup Match is won by the U.S. women amateurs.

1934 The Masters is founded by Bobby Jones. The PGA begins keeping extensive records of professional golfing events.

1944 The Women's Professional Golf Association is founded—the forerunner of the Ladies Professional Golf Association (LPGA).

1945 Byron Nelson wins eleven consecutive titles.

1945 Sam Snead and Ben Hogan return to the links after the war.

1946 The first Women's PGA Championship is held.

1950 Babe Didrikson Zaharias wins five out of nine tournaments in the first season of the LPGA.

1955 The first USGA Senior Men's Championship is held.

1963 Arnold Palmer becomes the first golfer to earn six figures.

1965 Sam Snead, age fifty-two, wins the Greensboro Open, capping his eighty-four tournament wins.

1970 Jack Nicklaus becomes the first golfer to earn $1 million in his career.

1971 Captain Alan Shepard of *Apollo 14* plays golf on the moon.

1977 An historic neck-and-neck duel takes place between Tom Watson and Jack Nicklaus at the British Open, which Watson wins.

1980   The Senior PGA tour is initiated by Deane Beman, the PGA commissioner.

1981   Kathy Whitworth becomes the first woman golfer to earn $1 million in her career.

1992   Tiger Woods, sixteen years old, plays the in Nissan Los Angeles Open.

1996   Tiger Woods turns professional and signs for $60 million in endorsement deals.

1997   Tiger Woods, at twenty-one, wins the Masters by twelve strokes, the widest margin of victory in the tournament's sixty-three-year history.

Three Great Golf Shots

1. In 1935, in the Masters at Augusta, Gene Sarazen hit a double eagle on the par-5 fifteenth hole in the final round. In doing so, he forced a tie with Craig Wood, winning the play-off the next day.

2. In 1982, in the U.S. Open at Pebble Beach, on the par-3 seventeenth hole, Tom Watson hit his first shot into the rough off the green. In "the shot heard 'round the world," Watson chipped in the second shot for a birdie. His subsequent birdie on the eighteenth gave him a come-from-behind victory to defeat Jack Nicklaus. He reportedly said to his caddie before doing so, "I'm going to make it."

3. In the 1987 Masters, Larry Mize, an unknown hometown boy who had won only one Tour event to date, shot a final round 71 to force a sudden-death play-off with Seve Ballesteros and Greg Norman. At the second extra hole, Mize played a chip shot from 140 feet for a birdie and a win.

Three Great Rounds of Golf

1. In a three-way play-off with British greats Ted Ray and Harry Vardon at the 1913 U.S. Open, at the Country Club in Brookline, Massachusetts, Francis Ouimet shot a 72 (compared to Vardon's 77 and Ray's 78) to win the tournament and put America on the golfing map.

2. In the second round of the Danny Thomas–Memphis Classic, at the Colonial Country Club, Al Geiberger shot eleven birdies and one eagle and finished with a 13-under-par 59, becoming the only man to hit below 60 in a tournament.

3. In the 1973 U.S. Open, at Oakmont in Pennsylvania, Johnny Miller shot a final round 63 to win the day.

The Biggest Flub in Tournament History

In 1968, on the seventy-first hole in the Masters at Augusta, Roberto de Vicenzo's playing partner, Tommy Aaron, inadvertently wrote down a four rather than a birdie 3 on the scorecard for de Vicenzo. De Vicenzo signed it and the score had to stand. Bob Goalby defeated him by one stroke.

3

The Golfers Hall of Fame

When it comes to the game of life, I figure I've
played the whole course.
> —LEE TREVINO

If this is how he is every week, then it's over. He's
the greatest player in the history of the game.
> —PETER JACOBSEN (on Tiger Woods, after he
> placed fifth, third, first, third, and first in a
> series of tournaments soon after turning pro)

The following is a listing of some of the great golfers of history.
You'll see that as I've gotten closer to the present, I've become
more liberal in my accolades, with a win in one of the majors
qualifying a golfer to be listed—after all, these active golfers
might win a biggie again.

Male Golfers

Willie Anderson (Scottish born; moved to United States): For winning the U.S. Open three years in a row, from 1903 to 1905.

Isao Aoki (Japanese): For winning the 1983 European Open and for being the first golfer from Japan to win on the U.S. Tour (in the 1983 Hawaiian Open).

Tommy Armour (Scottish born; moved to United States): For winning the U.S. Open in 1927, the U.S. PGA Championship in 1930, and the British Open in 1931; and for his classic instructional book, *How to Play Your Best Golf All the Time.*

Paul Azinger (American): For winning the PGA Championship in 1993.

John Ball (British): For being the first Englishman to win the British Open, in 1890, ending a twenty-nine-year run (beginning with the first Open in 1850) by Scotsmen.

Seve Ballesteros (Spanish): For winning the British Open in 1979, 1984, and 1988, and the Masters in 1980 and 1983; and for becoming the first golfer to earn more than £1 million on the European Tour, in 1986.

Frank Beard (American): For being top money winner on the U.S. Tour in 1969.

Julius Boros (American): For winning the U.S. Open in 1952 and 1963 (at the age of forty-three), and for being top money winner on the U.S. Tour in 1952 and 1955.

The title of the chapter refers to this book's version of a Hall of Fame—not the PGA's. Nor does it refer to the World Golf Hall of Fame, established in Pinehurst, North Carolina, which, by 1998, will be part of the World Golf Village, eight miles north of St. Augustine, Florida.

James Braid (Scottish): For winning five British Opens between 1901 and 1910.

Gay Brewer (American): For winning eleven U.S. Tour events, including the 1967 Masters and the 1972 Canadian Open.

Mark Calcavecchia (American): For winning the British Open in 1989.

Billy Casper (American): For his more than fifty U.S. Tour wins from the 1950s to the 1970s, including the U.S. Open in 1959 and 1966 and the Masters in 1989; and for being top money winner on the U.S. Tour in 1966 and 1968.

Bob Charles (New Zealander): For being the only left-hander—a category I'm partial to—to win the British Open (1963).

Harry Cooper (British born; moved to United States): For winning twenty U.S. Tour events between 1923 and 1943—nine of those events in 1937, making him top money winner that year.

Henry Cotton (British): For being the only man to win the British Open both before (1934 and 1937) and after (1948) the Second World War.

Fred Couples (American): For winning the Masters in 1992 and being top money winner on the U.S. Tour that year.

Bruce Crampton (Australian): For becoming the first Australian to earn more than $1 million on the U.S. Tour, in 1973.

Ben Crenshaw (American): For winning the Masters in 1984 and 1995.

John Daly (American): For winning the PGA Championship in 1991 and the British Open in 1995 (and for his 300-yard-long drives).

Jimmy Demaret (American): For winning six tournaments, including the Masters, in one year (1940); also for winning the Masters two more times (1947 and 1950), to become the first three-time winner; and for winning all three foursomes and all three singles in the Ryder Cup competitions in 1947, 1949, and 1951.

Roberto de Vicenzo (Argentinian): For finishing in the top three eight times between 1948 and 1969; and for winning 150 professional tournaments, including the 1967 British Open.

Bruce Devlin (Australian): For winning the Australian, New Zealand, and French Open titles in 1963.

Leo Diegel (American): For winning two successive PGA titles in 1928 and 1929; for winning the Canadian Open four times; and for winning more than thirty tournaments in his career.

Olin Dutra (American): For winning the PGA title in 1932 and the U.S. Open in 1934, and for his career twenty-one tournament wins.

Ernie Els (South African): For winning the U.S. Open in 1994.

Nick Faldo (British): For winning the British PGA Championship in 1978, 1980, and 1981; the British Open in 1987, 1990, and 1992; and the Masters in 1989, 1990, and 1996.

Jim Ferrier (Australian born; became U.S. citizen): For winning the Australian Open twice; for being the first Australian winner of the PGA Championship in 1947; and for winning twenty-one U.S. Tour events between 1944 and 1961.

Raymond Floyd (American): For winning the PGA Championship in 1969 and 1982, and for becoming the oldest golfer to win the U.S. Open, in 1986, at the age of forty-three.

Ed Furgol (American): For playing with a disabled left arm throughout his career and winning the U.S. Open in 1954.

Al Geiberger (American): For becoming the first man to break 60 in a U.S. Tour event, at the Danny Thomas–Memphis Classic at the Colonial Country Club in 1977 (he is known as Mister 59); for eleven U.S. Tour wins between 1962 and 1979; and for winning the 1966 PGA Championship.

David Graham (Australian): For winning the PGA Championship in 1979 and the U.S. Open in 1981.

Hubert Green (American): For ninteen U.S. Tour wins, including the 1977 U.S. Open and the 1985 PGA Championship (following surgery for a shoulder injury).

Ralph Gudahl (American): For winning back-to-back U.S. Opens in 1937 and 1938 and the Masters in 1939.

Walter Hagen (American): For winning the U.S. Open in 1914 and 1919; the British Open in 1922, 1924, 1928, and 1929; the PGA Championship in 1921, 1924, 1925, 1926, and 1927; the French Open in 1920; and the Australian Open in 1931.

Harold Hilton (British): For becoming the first player to win the U.S. and British amateur titles in the same year (1911).

Ben Hogan (American): For sixty-two U.S. Tour wins, including nine majors (the U.S. Open four times, the Masters twice, the PGA Championship twice, and the British Open once). In 1953 he won the Masters, the U.S. Open, and the British Open, becoming the first man to win three majors in a year. (In 1949 he had been involved in a serious auto accident in which he suffered a broken collarbone and fractured pelvis.)

Jock Hutchison (Scottish born; moved to United States): For winning the Western Open in 1920 and 1923; for being PGA Championship in 1920; and for being the first American, in 1921, to win the British Open (in successive holes at St. Andrews, in his country of birth, he scored a hole-in-one and a two).

Hale Irwin (American): For winning the U.S. Open in 1974, 1979, and 1990.

Tony Jacklin (British): For winning the 1969 British Open (the first British player to do so in eighteen years) and the 1970 U.S. Open (the first British player to do so in thirty years).

Don January (American): For winning the PGA Championship in 1967; for eleven U.S. Tour wins; and for winning the Tournament of Champions on the regular tour and the Seniors Tournament of Champions in the same year (1987).

Lee Janzen (American): For winning the U.S. Open in 1993.

Bobby Jones (American): For winning thirteen majors as an amateur during a short career (1923–30); for winning the U.S. Amateur and British Amateur championships and the U.S. Open and British Open in a single year (1930), the first "Grand Slam"; and for helping to design Augusta and found the Masters in 1934.

Tom Kite (American): For being top money winner on the U.S. Tour in 1981 and for winning the U.S. Open in 1992.

Bernhard Langer (German): For winning the Masters in 1985 and 1993.

Tony Lema (American): For winning the British Open in 1964 and for being the third man, after Jack Nicklaus and Arnold Palmer, to win more than $100,000 in a season.

Lawson Little (American): For winning both the U.S. Amateur and British Amateur titles two years in a row, 1934 and 1935, and the U.S. Open in 1940.

Gene Littler (American): For winning the Tournament of Champions three years in a row, in 1955, 1956, and 1957, and the U.S. Open in 1961; and for his twenty-nine U.S. Tour wins.

Bobby Locke (South African): For winning eighty tournaments worldwide, including the South African Open nine times between 1935 and 1955, and the British Open in 1949, 1950, 1952, and 1957.

Liang-Huan Lu (Taiwanese): For dominating the Asian circuit in the 1960s and 1970s; for winning the French Open in 1971; and for helping Taiwan win the World Cup in 1972.

Sandy Lyle (British): For winning the British Open in 1985 and the Masters in 1988.

John McDermott (American): For being the youngest winner of the U.S. Open in 1911 (age nineteen) and winning again in 1912.

Arnaud Massy (French): For winning the French Open in 1906 and 1907, the British Open in 1907, and the Spanish Open in 1912 and 1928.

Phil Mickelson (American): For winning the NCAA golf title three times, the U.S. Amateur Championship in 1990, and a number of U.S. Tour events since then; and for doing it all left-handed—once again, my particular bias.

Cary Middlecoff (American): For winning the U.S. Open in 1949 and 1956; five U.S. Tour events in 1955, including the Masters; and thirty-seven Tour wins overall.

Johnny Miller (American): For winning the U.S. Open in 1973, fourteen U.S. Tour events between 1974 and 1976, and the British Open in 1976; and for being top money winner on the U.S. Tour in 1974.

Larry Mize (American): For winning the Masters in 1987 as an unknown hometown Augusta boy.

Orville Moody (American): For winning the 1969 U.S. Open— he is part Choctaw Indian and, as such, the only Native American to win a major.

Tom Morris (Scottish): For winning four British Opens in the

1860s. (His son, Young Tom Morris, took up where Old Tom Morris left off.)

Kel Nagle (Australian): For winning the New Zealand Open in 1957 and 1958; the Australian Open in 1960; the British Open in 1960; and the Canadian Open in 1964.

Tsuneyaki (Tommy) Nakajima (Japanese): For winning the Japan PGA title three times and the Japan Open twice in the 1970s and 1980s.

Byron Nelson (American): For winning fifty-four U.S. Tour events (twenty-six between 1944 and 1945), including the Masters in 1937 and 1942, the U.S. Open in 1939, and the PGA Championship in 1940 and 1945.

Larry Nelson (American): For winning the PGA Championship in 1981 and 1987 and the U.S. Open in 1983.

Jack Nicklaus (American): For winning a record eighteen majors from 1962 to 1986 (the year of his fourth Masters win, at age forty-three); for being top money winner on the U.S. Tour a record eight times, between 1964 and 1976; for being the PGA Player of the Year five times, between 1967 and 1976; and for being awarded the U.S. Athlete of the Decade Award in 1980.

Greg Norman (Australian): For being top money winner on the U.S. Tour in 1986 and 1990, and for winning the British Open in 1986 and 1993.

Christy O'Connor (Irish): For winning twenty-four European tournaments between 1955 and 1972.

José María Olazabal (Spanish): For winning the Masters in 1994.

Peter Oosterhuis (British): For winning the Vardon Trophy four years in succession in the early 1970s; for being selected for the Ryder Cup team every year between 1971 and 1981; and for winning the Canadian Open in 1981.

Francis Ouimet (American): For winning the U.S. Open in 1913 and the U.S. Amateur title in 1914 and 1931.

Arnold Palmer (American): For sixty-one U.S. Tour wins from the 1950s into the 1970s, including the Masters four times, the British Open twice, and the U.S. Open once; for being the first player to win $1 million on the U.S. Tour (and being top money winner four times); and for being the first television golf hero, bringing the game of golf gracefully into a new era.

Willie Park (Scottish): For winning the first British Open in 1860, and three others later; and for being the first professional golfer to write a book about the sport, *The Game of Golf*. (His son—also Willie Park—won two British Opens, in 1887 and 1889.)

Jerry Pate (American): For winning the U.S. Open and Canadian Open in 1976 and for earning more than $1 million by age twenty-seven.

Corey Pavin (American): For winning the U.S. Open in 1995 and for being top money winner on the U.S. Tour in 1991.

Calvin Peete (American): For his twelve U.S. Tour wins between 1979 and 1986—and for competing successfully, as an African American, at a time when racial prejudice was even more overt than it is now.

Henry Picard (American): For winning twenty-seven U.S. Tour events between 1934 and 1945, including the 1938 Masters and the 1939 PGA Championship.

Gary Player (South African): For winning the South African Open thirteen times; for being World Match-Play Champion five times, between 1965 and 1973; and for winning the

Arnold Palmer

British Open three times, the Masters three times, the U.S. Open once, and the PGA Championship once.

Nick Price (born in South Africa of English parents; moved to United States): For winning the PGA Championship in 1992 and 1994 and the British Open in 1994, and for being top money winner on the U.S. Tour in 1993.

Ted Ray (British): For winning the British Open in 1912 and the U.S. Open in 1920.

Doug Sanders (American): For winning twenty U.S. Tour events in the 1950s and 1970s. (Who says you have to win one of the majors to be appreciated?)

Gene Sarazen (American): For winning the U.S. Open in 1922 and 1932; the PGA Championship in 1922, 1923, and 1933; the British Open in 1932; and the Masters in 1935.

Denny Shute (American): For winning the British Open in 1933 and the PGA Championship in 1936 and 1937.

Horton Smith (American): For winning thirty U.S. Tour events between 1928 and 1941, including the Masters in 1934 and 1936.

Sam Snead (American): For winning 84 U.S. Tour events and an estimated 135 worldwide, including three Masters (one in 1954 at age forty-one), three PGA Championships, and one British Open.

Craig Stadler (American): For winning the Tucson Open, Masters, Kemper Open, and World Series of Golf all in 1982, the year he was top money winner on the U.S. Tour.

Payne Stewart (American): For winning the PGA Championship in 1989 and the U.S. Open in 1991.

Dave Stockton (American): For winning the PGA Championship in 1970 and 1976.

Curtis Strange (American): For winning the U.S. Open in 1988 and 1989 and for being top money winner on the U.S. Tour in 1985, 1987, and 1988.

Hal Sutton (American): For being top money winner on the U.S. Tour in 1983 and winning the PGA Championship that year.

John Henry Taylor (British): For winning five British Opens at the turn of the century.

Peter Thomson (Australian): For winning five British Opens between 1954 and 1965, the New Zealand Open nine times, and the Australian Open three times.

Lee Trevino (American): For winning the U.S. Open, the PGA Championship, and the British Open twice each; for winning the U.S., British, and Canadian Opens within a three-week period, in 1971; and for being top money winner on the U.S. Tour in 1970.

Bob Tway (American): For winning the PGA Championship in 1986.

Harry Vardon (British): For winning six British Opens at the turn of the century.

Ken Venturi (American): For fourteen U.S. Tour wins, including the 1964 U.S. Open.

Lanny Wadkins (American): For winning the PGA Championship in 1977 and numerous other Tour wins.

Tom Watson (American): For winning eight majors between 1975 and 1983, including five British Opens, two Masters, and one U.S. Open; and for being top money winner on the U.S. Tour for four years, from 1977 to 1980.

Tom Weiskopf (American): For winning fifteen U.S. Tour events, including the 1973 British Open.

Tiger Woods (American): For winning the 1997 Masters in

record fashion, for winning three consecutive U.S. Amateur Championships, and for turning the golf world upside down with his awesome talent and "rainbow gallery."

Ian Woosnam (British): For winning the PGA Championship in 1988 and the Masters in 1991.

Fuzzy Zoeller (American): For winning the Masters in 1979 and the U.S. Open in 1984.

Female Golfers

I think I can say with safety that woman's championship golf has not only come to stay but that it's sure to keep growing all the way from here on in.

—NANCY LOPEZ

Amy Alcott (American): For winning the U.S. Women's Open in 1980 and numerous other U.S. Tour wins.

Patty Berg (American): For winning more than eighty events and being top money winner in 1954, 1955, and 1957; and for founding the LPGA in 1949 with Betty Jameson, Louise Suggs, Mickey Wright, and Babe Didrikson Zaharias.

Susie Maxwell Berning (American): For winning the U.S. Women's Open in 1968, 1972, and 1973.

Pat Bradley (American): For winning more than thirty events, including the U.S. Women's Open in 1981, and for being top money winner in 1986 and 1991.

Jerilyn Britz (American): For winning the U.S. Women's Open in 1979.

Donna Caponi (American): For winning the U.S. Women's Open in 1969 and 1970.

JoAnne Gunderson Carner (American): For winning forty-two events, including the U.S. Women's Open in 1971 and 1976, and for being top money winner in 1974, 1982, and 1983.

Beth Daniel (American): For being top money winner in 1980 and 1981.

Laura Davies (British): For winning ten events, including the U.S. Women's Open in 1987 and the LPGA Championship in 1994 and 1996.

Betty Jameson (American): For winning the U.S. Women's Amateur Championship in 1939 and 1940, and for founding the LPGA with Patty Berg, Louise Suggs, Mickey Wright, and Babe Didrikson Zaharias.

Betsy King (American): For winning more than twenty events between 1984 and 1990, including the U.S. Women's Open in 1989 and 1990; and for being top money winner in 1984, 1989, and 1993.

Nancy Lopez (American): For winning more than forty-five events, including the LPGA Championship three times (1978, 1985, and 1989); for being top money winner in 1978, 1979, and 1985; and for being a four-time Player of the Year.

Meg Mallon (American): For winning six events, including the U.S. Women's Open in 1991.

Laurie Merton (American): For winning the U.S. Women's Open in 1993.

Liselotte Neumann (Swedish): For winning the U.S. Women's Open in 1988.

Ayako Okamoto (Japanese): For being top money winner in 1987.

Sandra Palmer (American): For winning the U.S. Women's Open in 1975 and being top money winner that year.

Dottie Pepper (American): For being top money winner in 1992.

Judy Rankin (American): For being top money winner in 1976 and 1977.

Betsy Rawls (American): For winning the U.S. Women's Open in 1951, 1953, 1957, and 1960; and for being top money winner in 1952 and 1959.

Patty Sheehan (American): For winning the U.S. Women's Open in 1992 and 1994.

Annika Sorenstam (Swedish): For winning the U.S. Women's Open in 1995 and 1996, and for being Player of the Year in 1995 and 1996.

Hollis Stacy (American): For winning the U.S. Women's Open in 1977, 1978, and 1984.

Louise Suggs (American): For winning the U.S. Women's Open in 1949 and 1952; for being top money winner in 1953 and 1960; and for founding the LPGA with Patty Berg, Betty Jameson, Mickey Wright, and Babe Didrikson Zaharias.

Sherri Turner (American): For being top money winner in 1988.

Kathy Whitworth (American): For winning eighty-eight events, including six majors, and for being top money winner a record eight times, between 1965 and 1973.

Mickey Wright (American): For winning eighty-two events, including the U.S. Women's Open in 1958, 1959, 1961, and 1964; for being top money winner four years in a row, from 1961 to 1964; and for founding the LPGA with Patty Berg, Betty Jameson, Louise Suggs, and Babe Didrikson Zaharias.

Babe Didrikson Zaharias (American): For winning thirty-one events and ten majors in an eight-year period, including the U.S. Women's Open in 1948, 1950, and 1954; for being top money winner for four years in a row, from 1948 to 1951; and for being a founder of the LPGA.

4

Other Golf Notables: Coaches, Course Designers, and Celebrities

I'm the best. I just haven't played yet.
—MUHAMMAD ALI (about his golf game)

The constellation of golf notables includes others besides professional golfers. In this chapter we'll take a look at some of them.

Some Famous Coaches

If you expect a miracle, you should expect to pay for one.
—DEREK HARDY (a teaching pro, discussing why he charges $140 for a series of thirteen lessons, but demands $1,000 for a single lesson)

Jim Flick   Jim Flick has worked in the *Golf Digest* golf school program with Bob Toski. He has coached Susie Maxwell Berning, Hollis Stacy, Tom Lehman, and Andrew Magee, among others.

Butch Harmon   Butch Harmon has coached Greg Norman, Davis Love III, and Tiger Woods, among others. He works out of the Lochinvar Golf Club in Houston, Texas.

Peter Kostis   Peter Kostis works out of the Kostis/McCord Learning Center in Scottsdale, Arizona, with Gary McCord.

David Leadbetter   David Leadbetter helped Nick Faldo, among many others. He works out of Lake Nona Golf Club in Orlando, Florida.

Gary McCord   A former PGA Tour member and a commentator with CBS Sports, Gary McCord works out of the Kostis/McCord Learning Center, with Peter Kostis.

Harvey Penick   Harvey Penick worked with numerous golfing greats. He is known for his books as well, the first of which was *Harvey Penick's Little Red Book: Lessons and Teachings for a Lifetime in Golf.*

Dean Reinmuth   Dean Reinmuth heads his own school of golf in San Diego, California. He has worked with Phil Mickelson, among others.

Bob Rotella   Dr. Bob Rotella is a sports psychologist and performance consultant who has worked with Pat Bradley, Brad Faxon, Tom Kite, and Nick Price, among others. He is the director of sports psychology at the University of Virginia.

Fred Shoemaker Fred Shoemaker specializes in golf's inner game. His School for Extraordinary Golf is in Carmel Valley, California.

Bob Toski   Bob Toski works out of the Toski-Battersby International Golf Center in Coconut Creek, Florida. He has worked in the *Golf Digest* golf school program.

Gary Wiren   Dr. Gary Wiren is the master teacher at the PGA National Golf Club in Palm Beach Gardens, Florida.

There are many other less costly teachers of golf. You might want to look into golf schools or talk to the local club pros or driving-range pros.

Some Famous Course Designers

Henry Colt   Henry Colt redesigned the Old Course at Sunningdale in England (originally designed by Willie Park Jr.) and built the New Course there, among others. His courses are known for demanding accuracy and strategy.

Pete Dye   An American architect, Pete Dye is known for his challenging courses—more than seventy-three of them. In South Carolina he designed Harbour Town Links on Hilton Head Island, as well as the Ocean Course at Kiawah Island; in Florida, the PGA Tournament Players' Course at Sawgrass; and, in California, the PGA West Stadium Course at La Quinta (where the seventeenth hole is called Alcatraz). On these courses and others, he worked with his wife, Alice Dye. He worked with Jack Nicklaus, as well, on Harbour Town.

Bobby Jones   Jones's most famous work in golf course design was at Augusta National, with Alister Mackenzie.

Robert Trent Jones Sr.   Robert Trent Jones was born in England, but moved to the United States at the age of four. He designed the second course at Ballybunion, in County Kerry, Ireland; Kananaskis, in Alberta, Canada; Quinta de Marinha, in Portugal; the Dunes, in South Carolina; the Robert Trent Jones Golf Club, in Lake Manassas, Virginia; and Spyglass Hill, in Pebble Beach, California. He also remodeled the Augusta National Golf Club, the Baltusrol Golf Club, the Firestone Country Club, the Oak Hill Country Club, the Oakland Hills Country Club, the Oakmont Country Club, and the Olympic Club. His sons also are course designers.

Charles Blair MacDonald An American, MacDonald studied British course design while at school in England. In 1895 he built the first eighteen-hole course in the United States, at the Chicago Golf Club in Illinois. He also built the National Golf Links at Southampton, Long Island in New York.

Alister Mackenzie Mackenzie studied under Henry Colt. He is most famous for his work with Bobby Jones. He also designed Cypress Point, in California, and redesigned the West Course at Royal Melbourne, in Australia.

Tom Morris Old Tom Morris, who was a golfer and a greenskeeper both, was also the first great course designer. Muirfield and Royal Dornach, in Scotland, and Royal County Down, in Ireland, are some of his creations.

Jack Nicklaus Nicklaus designed Harbour Town Links, in South Carolina, with Pete and Alice Dye, and Muirfield Village, in Ohio with Desmond Muirhead. He also designed Glen Abbey, in Ontario, among others.

Willie Park Jr. Winner of two British Opens, Park became known for his work as a course designer with the Old Course at Sunningdale, in England.

Donald Ross Born in Scotland, Ross designed many courses in the United States, including Oakland Hills, in Michigan, and Pinehurst Number 2, in North Carolina.

Tom Simpson Simpson is known for designing Chantilly, in France, and other European courses.

Dick Wilson Wilson worked with a lot of other golf architects before designing Doral and Pine Tree, both in Florida, and Royal Montreal, in Canada, among others.

Some Celebrity Golfers

The safest place would be the fairway.

—Joe Garagiola (on where the gallery should
stand during a celebrity tournament)

Course Crooning

Bing Crosby loved the game of golf and founded the Bing
Crosby National Pro-Am. It's played on a variety of courses,
most notably Pebble Beach, Cypress Point, and Spyglass Hill.

Comedian First, Golfer Second

Bob Hope was gaga over golf and spent much of his leisure
time on the links. He owned a $12,000 golf cart in his like-
ness—its front showed his famous nose and chin. He helped
promote the Bob Hope–Chrysler Classic, and his association
with golf gave him lots of ammo for his comedy routines. For
example, he once said of Sammy Davis Jr.: "He hits the ball
130 yards and his jewelry goes 150." He also could joke about
his own game: "He [Arnold Palmer] has won almost as much
money playing golf as I've spent on lessons." It's good he
could joke about his game, because as Jimmy Demaret pointed
out: "Bob has a beautiful short game. Unfortunately, it's off
the tee." Hope once said: "I'll shoot my age if I have to live
to be 105."

Once, when he was playing producer Sam Goldwyn at Lakeside Country Club, Hope discreetly retrieved a club Goldwyn
had tossed in a bush in reaction to missing a 2-foot putt, slipping it into his own bag. On the next green, Hope used the
putter and managed to sink a 20-footer. Goldwyn, impressed,

asked to borrow the putter. He liked its feel so much he offered to buy it. Hope charged Goldwyn $50 for his own putter.

Keeping One's Priorities Straight

Jack Benny loved golf, but not beyond reason: "Give me good clubs, fresh air, and a beautiful partner, and you can keep the clubs and fresh air."

Not Really Recommended

In one take for the 1938 film *Carefree*, excellent golfer Fred Astaire hit twelve golf balls while dancing. They all landed within eight feet of each other.

The Great Debate

Will Rogers loved golf and spoke of it often: "Golf is good for the soul. You get so mad at yourself you forget to hate your enemies." But how good for the soul? "Golf has made more liars out of people than the income tax."

Hackers and Streakers

Harpo Marx and George Burns once caused a ruckus at the Hillcrest Country Club in Beverly Hills, when they played a round of golf in their underwear.

A Really Good Show

Groucho Marx, who loved golf but never broke 90, hit five tee shots in a row into the Pacific on the infamous sixteenth hole at Cypress Point, in a match against Ed Sullivan. Rather than tee up a sixth time, Groucho picked up his golf bag, carried it to the edge of the cliff, and tossed it into the ocean. His expla-

Nancy Lopez

nation: "It's not that I'm a poor loser, but I figured if I couldn't beat a fellow with no neck, I've got to be the world's worst golfer and I have no right to be on a course at all."

Don't Forget Zeppo

Zeppo Marx once said, "The hardest shot is a mashie at ninety yards from the green where the ball has to be played against an oak tree, bounces back into a sand trap, hits a stone, bounces on the green, and then rolls into the cup. That shot is so difficult I have only made it once."

A Healthy Dose of Realism

When asked by Toots Shor what to give the caddie after Shor shot 211, Jackie Gleason replied, "Your clubs."

Religion 101

Senator Adlai Stevenson once said: "Some of us worship in churches, some in synagogues, some on golf courses."

Don't Waste Your Words

The Reverend Billy Graham took pleasure in a golf game, but, as he said, "Prayer never seems to work for me on the golf course. I think this has something to do with my being a terrible putter."

And Who Might You Be?

Baseball great Babe Ruth was a dedicated golfer who could whack a ball but couldn't remember his partner's name, calling just about everyone "kid"—even if he was speaking to a golf pro.

It Couldn't Have Happened to a Nicer Guy

Mobster Al Capone accidentally shot himself in the foot with a gun hidden in his golf bag at Burnham Woods Golf Course in 1928—giving a new meaning to the term *hole-in-one.*

A Real Lemmon

Actor Jack Lemmon is famous for his lousy golf. For twenty-five straight years he failed to make the cut at the Bing Crosby Pro-Am. Byron Nelson once said of Lemmon's swing, "My God, he looks like he's beating a chicken." Peter Jacobsen expressed it this way: "I've seen better swings on a condemned playground." Comedian Phil Harris quipped, "Jack Lemmon's been in more bunkers than Eva Braun." Lemmon himself once remarked, "I would rather open on Broadway in *Hamlet,* with no rehearsals, than tee off at Pebble Beach in the tournament."

Golf and Masochism

Phyllis Diller has suffered through many a golf game: "Golf has taught me there is a connection between pain and pleasure. *Golf* spelled backwards is *flog.*"

What Game Are We Playing Here?

Ole Blue Eyes and Arnold Palmer were playing together for the first time in Palm Springs. Sinatra kept ending up in the rough. After the round, Sinatra queried Palmer on what he thought of his game. Palmer replied, "Not bad, but I still prefer golf."

Drinking and Driving

Dean Martin loved golf and referred to it often in his humor: "If you drink, don't drive. Don't even putt." In reference to some fans in the gallery, he once said, "You've heard of Arnie's Army. Well, those are Dean's Drunks."

A Singing Fool

The singer Johnny Mathis had a bad outing at Moor Allerton in Yorkshire, England. Teeing off, he lost four balls in a row. The fifth ball ended in the bush, but it still could be played. As he walked along the fairway, Mathis suddenly broke into loud song. When his partners looked at him in surprise, he said, "Thank God, I can still sing."

Do That Again, Please

Basketball player Hot Rod Hundley added a new dimension to the game in the 1986 Showdown Classic Pro-Am at the Jeremy Ranch Golf Club in Park City, Utah. On the second tee, his first shot slammed into the ground and created a cloud of dust—the ball only rolled a few feet forward, but then, because of spin, it reversed itself and rolled back past Hundley's feet. On the second shot, he cold-topped the ball, causing it to roll as far as the tee markers. On the third shot, the ball went straight up over his head about twenty feet. Hot Rod stuck out his right hand and casually caught the ball as if this were a trick shot.

A Regular Guy

President Woodrow Wilson always played golf in street shoes.

Perks of the Office

President Dwight Eisenhower had a green on the White House lawn. When asked about how his golf game changed after leaving the White House, Ike replied, "A lot more people beat me now."

But He's There to Protect You

Upon being asked why he objected to pictures being taken of him playing golf when President Eisenhower had permitted them, President John Kennedy said, "It is true that my predecessor did not object as I do to pictures of one's golfing skills in action. But neither, on the other hand, did he ever bean a Secret Service agent."

I Am Not a Crook

In reference to President Richard Nixon, Sam Snead once said, "Nixon could relate to the ordinary guy who plays. Hell, I even once caught him cheating a little bit—moving the ball when he didn't think nobody could see him. All hackers do that."

That's One Way to Rate Your Game

When asked about his game, President Gerald Ford replied, "I know I'm getting better at golf because I'm hitting fewer spectators." As Bob Hope put it, "It's not hard to find Gerald Ford on a golf course. Just follow the wounded."

Presidential Yips

Ken Raynor, the club pro at the Kennebunkport course, in speaking about President George Bush, said: "He'd rather face Congress than a three-foot putt."

A Vote of Confidence

Tommy Bolt stated that President Bill Clinton "told me he caddied in the same group with me in the Hot Springs Open. That's why I voted for him, because he was my caddie." (In fact, Clinton may be the best presidential golfer ever. Greg Norman, for one, observed that Clinton would "break eighty every time" if he had more time to practice.

It Sort of Makes Sense

Yogi Berra is famous for pithy, almost-logical statements, as in "Ninety percent of putts that are short don't go in."

It's All in the Wrists

Hank Aaron loved to play golf, but as he said after a frustrating day on the links, "It took me seventeen years to get three thousand hits in baseball. I did it in one afternoon on the golf course."

A Fine Line, but All the Difference in the World

Chicago Cubs great Ernie Banks once said, "Baseball reveals character; golf exposes it."

Let's Not Mince Words

Baseball player George Brett hit the links often: "I was three over: one over a house; one over a patio, and one over a swimming pool."

Seven for Seven

On being asked how many days a week he played golf now that he was retired from basketball, Jerry West said, "Only on days ending in Y."

How Befitting

Sean Connery and historic seaside links courses on the British Isles go well together, wouldn't you say? As a case in point, the actor wrote the foreword to *The Scottish Golf Guide* by David Hamilton. Connery is a skilled and dedicated golf nut.

It May Not Pay the Bills, But . . .

Basketball player Charles Barkley knows how to keep his priorities straight. When asked about a shoulder injury, he said, "Man, the worst thing about this is I won't be able to play golf."

It Makes My Day

Clint Eastwood once said, "I couldn't tell you exactly what I like about golf. Just when you think you've got it mastered, it lets you know you haven't. I'm just crazy enough to do it."

Deceptively Hard

Football great Lawrence Taylor said it this way: "I like golf because I can go out and hit a little white ball that doesn't move and doesn't hit back. It should be easy, but it isn't."

A Committee of One

Willie Nelson knows the easiest route to improving one's golf game: "Par is whatever I say it is. I've got one hole that's a par-23, and yesterday I damn near birdied the sucker."

Now He's Even Crazier

Jack Nicholson said in reference to golf, "One minute it's fear and loathing, but hit a couple of good shots and you're on top of the world. I've gone crazy over this game."

Don't Be Like Mike

When asked about Michael Jordan's golf game, Peter Jacobsen said, "I'll be playing center for the Chicago Bulls before Michael Jordan plays on the Tour."

Not Bad for an Amateur

Kevin Costner likes to and can swing a golf club. Check him out on the silver screen in the movie *Tin Cup*. As part of the golfing community, he wrote the foreword to *Golf for Dummies*, by Gary McCord.

Tournament Time

In addition to the Bing Crosby National Pro-Am and the Bob Hope Desert Classic, other tournaments promoted by celebrities have been the Danny Thomas–Memphis Classic, the Glen Campbell Los Angeles Open, and, for women, the Dinah Shore Tournament.

More Celebrity Watching

Some celebrities spotted on the links over the years: President William Howard Taft, President Warren G. Harding, Jean Harlow, Rosalind Russell, Rita Hayworth, Clark Gable, Don Ameche, Oliver Hardy, Katharine Hepburn, Elizabeth Taylor, Arthur Ashe, and Bill Murray. In fact, if you have anything to do with politics or Hollywood or other professional sports and you've never golfed, you either are not successful enough to warrant any vacation time or you hang with the wrong crowd.

Lastly, If You Can't Beat Them, Why Not Just Join Them?

In 1981 Yul Brynner, who was going to do a series of shows of *The King and I* in Philadelphia, asked his agent to rent him a house where he could have some peace and quiet. His agent found him a place on Golf House Road, in the suburb of Ardmore. On his first Monday morning there, Brynner woke up to some noise outside. He looked out the window to see a crush of people. His agent had rented for him a house across from the Merion Golf Club . . . and the U.S. Open was just beginning.

5

Green Fields: Thirty-Six Historic and Beautiful Golf Courses

What a beautiful place a golf course is. From the meanest country pasture to the Pebble Beaches and St. Andrews of the world, a golf course is to me a holy ground. I feel God in the trees and grass and flowers, in the rabbits and the birds and the squirrels, in the sky and the water. I feel that I am home.

—HARVEY PENICK
(golf coach)

A good golf course makes you want to play so badly that you hardly have time to change your shoes.

—BEN CRENSHAW

One of the magical aspects of golf is that golf courses exist all over the world and no two are alike. The game and the experience vary significantly with the playing field. This is true of no other sport.

Here are some historic and beautiful courses you should know about (I've rounded off the number to eighteen in the United States and eighteen in the rest of the world—that number somehow appeals to me). You'll note that the last course listed is really the starting point in golf—Scotland's majestic St. Andrews.

A standard golf course is about 6,500 to 7,000 yards, with holes varying from 100 to 600 yards. There are more than 12,500 courses in the United States alone.

U.S. Courses

Augusta National—Augusta, Georgia

Designed by Alister Mackenzie and Bobby Jones in 1931. Home of the Masters. Known for its beauty and difficulty. The well-placed forty-six bunkers have determined a lot of titles. The eleventh, twelfth, and thirteenth holes are called the Amen Corner. Many pros have gone down swinging there over the decades. Those who survive them say, "Amen." One of golf's idyllic, holy places, Augusta is one of the truly great courses of the world.

Baltusrol—Springfield, New Jersey

The original course, owned by Louis Keller, the publisher of the *Social Register*, opened in 1895 and was completely redesigned by A. W. Tillinghast in 1922. With two courses, an upper and lower, Baltusrol has been the site of many U.S. championships, including seven U.S. Opens. The fourth hole, remodeled by Robert Trent Jones in preparation for the 1954 U.S. Open, is considered to be one of the best par-3 holes in the world, and the seventeenth is thought to be one of the best par-5s. The course is named after a Dutch farmer named Baltus Roll, who once owned the land. Jack Nicklaus won two of his four U.S. Opens (1967 and 1980) at Baltusrol.

The Country Club—Brookline, Massachusetts

Formally established in 1882, the Country Club became famous in 1913 when twenty-year-old American Francis Ouimet defeated the British greats Harry Vardon and Ted Ray in a three-way play-off.

Located in Brookline, just west of Boston, the tree-shaded course is one of America's oldest and stateliest.

Cypress Point—Monterey, California

Designed by Alister Mackenzie; opened in 1928. Located along the craggy shores of the Pacific Ocean, Cypress Point is considered by many to be one of the most beautiful golf courses in the world, especially the fifteenth, sixteenth, and seventeenth holes near the water's edge. The sixteenth hole is one of the most famous in all of golf—233 yards across an ocean inlet.

Doral—Miami, Florida

Designed by Dick Wilson in 1962. Doral, a popular resort and site of the Doral Open, has five championship courses, the most famous being the Blue course, known for its flat terrain and many lakes. That course's eighteenth hole, a 437-yard par-4, is known as the Blue Monster because of the water hazard running its entire left side.

Firestone—Akron, Ohio

Designed by Bertie Way; opened in 1929. Site of the World Series of Golf. In preparation for the 1960 PGA Championship, it was extensively remodeled by Robert Trent Jones. The sixteenth hole, a 625-yard par-5 is called the Monster—Arnold Palmer named it after a triple-bogey 8 in 1960.

Harbour Town Links—Hilton Head Island, South Carolina

Designed by Pete Dye and Jack Nicklaus in 1969. Site of the Heritage Golf Classic. It has tight fairways and small greens, challenging a golfer to find the right club for precision stroking. The par-4 eighteenth hole is famous because it requires two shots to carry water to reach the green. One of the teeing grounds for the eighteenth hole is rarely used in tournaments because it requires a drive of 250 yards to reach the fairway. It's known as the Nicklaus tee because it requires a drive like his.

Merion—Ardmore, Pennsylvania

Designed by Hugh Wilson; the present course opened in 1908. It is a short course known for slick greens, which were redesigned by Percy Maxwell in 1939 (otherwise the course is largely unchanged from its original design). Bobby Jones made his first U.S. Amateur appearance here at age fourteen in 1922; won his first Amateur title here in 1922; and won here again in 1930 to complete his famous Grand Slam. The thirteenth hole, a 129-yard par-3, is famous for its bunkers surrounding the green. Although it's a short course measuring only 6,500 yards, Jack Nicklaus said of Merion, "Acre for acre, it may be the best test of golf in the world."

Muirfield Village—Dublin, Ohio

Designed by Jack Nicklaus and Desmond Muirhead, Muirfield Village was the site of the 1992 U.S. Amateur Championship. Nicklaus named it after the famous Scottish course where he won his first British Open. The eighteenth hole, a 437-yard par-4 with numerous bunkers, has determined the outcome of a lot of events.

Oak Hill—Rochester, New York

Designed by Donald Ross in 1924; Robert Trent Jones remodeled it in 1956 and again in 1967. Known for its tall and numerous (forty thousand) trees and for its final three holes, par-5s normally, but par-4s when used in tournament play, Oak Hill has been the site of three U.S. Opens (1956, 1968, and 1989) and will host the U.S. Amateur in 1998.

Oakland Hills—Birmingham, Michigan

Designed by architect Donald Ross, who, upon seeing the land some eighteen miles northwest of Detroit in 1916, remarked, "The Lord intended this for a golf links." Oakland Hills opened in 1918 and was remodeled by Robert Trent Jones in 1951. Walter Hagen was its first club pro. Rolling wooded hills border the fairways; many of the greens are sloping. It has hosted six U.S. Opens (1924, 1937, 1951, 1961, 1985, and 1996), the last of which was won in dramatic fashion by Steve Jones.

Oakmont—Oakmont, Pennsylvania

Designed by Henry Fownes; opened in 1904 high above the Allegheny River outside Pittsburgh. Oakmont originally had 350 bunkers because Fownes felt that "A shot poorly played should be a shot irrevocably lost." To reduce maintenance costs, many were eliminated. The present number of sand traps is 171. A 60-yard-long bunker between the third and fourth holes, designed to entrap drives from both holes, is known as the Church Pews because it has seven grassy ridges in a row. Ben Hogan called the 453-yard par-4 fifteenth hole the most difficult he had ever played. Oakmont has hosted seven U.S. Opens (1927, 1935, 1953, 1962, 1973, 1983, and 1994)—Tommy Armour, Ben Hogan, Jack Nicklaus, and Johnny Miller have all won there.

The Olympic Club—San Francisco, California

Originally designed in the early twentieth century by Wilfred Reid; it was redesigned in 1924 by Sam Whiting and Willie Watson, who used several of the original holes; and redesigned again by Robert Trent Jones in the 1950s. Though short, Olympic is a difficult course because of the tall trees framing its holes, wet grass, and heavy rough. The sixteenth hole, a 605-yard par-5, is rarely birdied. Four U.S. Opens (1955, 1966, 1987, and 1998) have been sited at the fearsome Olympic, which writer Jim Murray labeled "a 6,700-yard haunted house. If it were human, it'd be Bela Lugosi."

Pebble Beach—Monterey, California

Initiated by Samuel Morse, nephew of the man who invented the telegraph, and designed by Jack Neville and Douglas Grant,

Pebble Beach opened in 1919. It is the site of the Bing Crosby National Pro-Am. Known for its thrilling beauty, its fourth through tenth holes overlook the Pacific Ocean. The eighteenth hole, a 548-yard par-5, is one of the most famous in golf, with the ocean situated to the left and out of bounds to the right—one often has to play the wind, hitting the ball out over the water. Home to the 1972, 1982, and 1992 U.S. Opens, it is the only public course to ever host an Open—Pinehurst, North Carolina, will share that distinction in 1999.

Pebble Beach has the highest greens fees in the United States: $275 per round.

Pine Valley—Clementon, New Jersey

Designed by George Crump in 1919. Pine Valley is famous for demanding distance and accuracy because of small landing areas and extensive expanses of sandy soil and scrub brush roughs and water hazards. A bunker on the seventh hole is called Hell's Half-Acre. It's the world's largest sand trap, extending 100 yards. Many consider Pine Valley to be the toughest course in the world.

Pinehurst (No. 2 Course)—Pinehurst, North Carolina

Designed by Donald Ross; opened in 1907. Site of the North and South Amateur. A subtle course, it has straight-ahead fairways lined with pine trees, with deceptively placed bunkers and small greens. Sam Snead calls it his "number one course," and it was rated ninth by *Golf Digest* on its 1995 list of America's 100 Greatest Golf Courses and sixth by *Golf* magazine.

Shinnecock Hills—Southampton, Long Island, New York

Designed by Scotsman Willie Davis in 1891. Shinnecock Indians helped build this course, the first eighteen-hole course in the United States. William Flynn and Howard Toomey remodeled it in 1931. The distinctive holes, sloping fairways, and ocean winds make Shinnecock Hills a very challenging course. The first clubhouse in the United States is Shinnecock Hill's, designed by the renowned New York architect Stanford White. The second U.S. Open was held at Shinnecock in 1896, and two men made forgotten history in the two-round tournament: John Shippen, an African-American caddie, finished tied for sixth (earning $10); and Oscar Bunn, a Shinnecock Indian caddie, came in twenty-first.

Each course has its own history, personality, and lingo. At Augusta National, the holes are named after flora: 1. Tea Olive, 2. Pink Dogwood, 3. Flowering Peach, 4. Flowering Crabapple, 5. Magnolia, 6. Juniper, 7. Pampas, 8. Yellow Jasmine, 9. Carolina Cherry, 10. Camelia, 11. White Dogwood, 12. Golden Bell, 13. Azalea, 14. Chinese Fir, 15. Fire Thorn, 16. Red Bud, 17. Nandina, and 18. Holly.

Outside the United States

Banff Springs—Banff, Alberta, Canada

Designed by Stanley Thompson in 1927. Located in the Rocky Mountains and known for its spectacular landscape and vistas.

The tenth hole at Pine Valley

Because of all the rock-blasting and earth-moving required to build this course, it was the first course to cost more than $1 million. The Banff Springs Hotel is a wonderful place to stay during a golfing vacation.

Ballybunion—County Kerry, Republic of Ireland

The Old Course was designed by a man named Murphy in 1896 and later remodeled by James Braid and Tom Simpson; the New Course was designed by Robert Trent Jones in 1985. Known as a stunningly beautiful traditional links (seaside) course and for its large sand dunes.

Carnoustie—Carnoustie, Scotland

Designed by Allan Robertson as a ten-hole course in 1839 and expanded to a full eighteen holes by James Braid in 1867. Remarkably, fifty-nine years later, the course was redesigned by Braid in 1926. Known for the variation in holes. They point in every direction. The Barry Burn crisscrosses the fairway on five holes, making it the most irksome stream in golf.

Castelconturbia—Novarra, Italy

Golf was first played here in 1898, and this course was the first host of the Italian Open in 1991. The first hole, a 562-yard par-5, is one of the most challenging first holes in Europe.

Chantilly—Chantilly, Oise, France

Designed by Tom Simpson at the turn of the century, and later redesigned because of damage during World War II. The course meanders through both woods and parkland. Considered by many to be France's best golf course, it is the site of many French Opens.

Fasterbo—Fasterbo, Fack, Sweden

Built as a nine-hole course in 1909; expanded to eighteen holes in 1930; redesigned in 1934. One of the few links (seaside courses) in mainland Europe, it has a lighthouse near the fourteenth green.

Fujioka—Nagoya, Japan

Designed by Peter Thomson and Michael Wolveridge; opened in 1971. Known for its use of water for both beauty and hazards and for its 605-yard par-5 sixteenth hole.

Glen Abbey—Oakville, Ontario, Canada

Designed by Jack Nicklaus in 1977. The permanent site of the Canadian Open. The Valley Holes, eleven through fourteen, are famous for determining championships.

Jasper Park—Jasper Park, Alberta, Canada

Designed by Stanley Thompson in 1925. Like Banff Springs, a spectacular mountain resort course, but with more tree-lined fairways.

Kananaskis—Kananaskis Village, Alberta, Canada

Designed by Robert Trent Jones in the early 1980s. Two public courses—Mount Lorette and Mount Kidd—in one location. Jones called the location in the Rocky Mountain foothills near Calgary, "the finest location" he'd ever seen for a golf course.

Muirfield—Muirfield, Lothian, Scotland

Moved to present location in 1891 where the course was designed by Old Tom Morris. The Honourable Company of

Edinburgh Golfers is the oldest golf organization. Its course at Muirfield, the oldest Open course still being used today (since 1892), is therefore steeped in tradition. Muirfield is not a true links course, not reaching as close to the sea as other Scottish courses; it is also flatter than most.

The National—Woodbridge, Ontario, Canada

Designed by George Fazio and Tom Fazio; opened in 1974. Canada's top-ranked course, it has beautiful rolling hills. The tenth through thirteenth holes are the most challenging.

Royal County Down—Newcastle, County Down, Northern Ireland

Designed by Old Tom Morris in 1889. A picturesque setting next to the sea with the Mountains of Mourne in the background. Royal County Down has five blind-tee shots—ask the caddie what to do.

Royal Dornoch—Dornoch, Sutherland, Scotland

Designed by Old Tom Morris in the late 1800s. Redesigned by John Sutherland, Donald Ross, and J. H. Taylor over the years. A traditional Scottish links (seaside) course.

Royal Hong Kong—Fanling, Hong Kong, China

The first course, the Old, was built in 1911; a second, the New, was built in 1931 (redesigned in 1968 by Michael Wolveridge); and a third course, the Eden, was built in 1970. The Old has a challenging stretch between the tenth and the thirteenth holes known as the Loop.

Royal Melbourne—Black Rock, Melbourne, Victoria, Australia

West Course opened in 1901 and was redesigned by Alister Mackenzie in 1926; East Course was designed by Alex Russell. A combination of the two courses is used in tournament play. Known for its quick greens and eucalyptus trees.

Royal Troon—Troon, Strathclyde, Scotland

Opened as a five-hole course in 1878; redesigned by Willie Fernie as an eighteen-hole course for play in 1888. Known for having one of the longest holes in British championship golf— the 577-yard par-5 sixth hole—and one of the shortest—the 125-yard par-3 eighth hole (the Postage Stamp).

St. Andrews—St. Andrews, Fife, Scotland

Established as the first eighteen-hole course in the mid-1700s. It is the holiest of holy golf courses, the home course of the Royal and Ancient, steeped in tradition—golf has been played there for four centuries. The Old Course, as it is often referred to, is known for its purity and simplicity. The seventeenth hole (some say the most difficult in the world) and the eighteenth hole, with the small stone Swilcan bridge, provide one of the most famous finishes in golf. The wind and the bunkers (such as Hell's Bunker) provide the greatest challenges.

6

Birdies, Bogeys, and Mulligans: A Brief Golfing Lexicon

That ghastly time when, with the first movement of the putter, the golfer blacks out, loses sight of the ball, and hasn't the remotest idea of what to do with the putter, or, occasionally, that he is holding a putter at all.

—TOMMY ARMOUR
(defining the "yips")

Okay, your address is all screwed up and you end up in bunkers and roughs. No eagle or birdies for you, much less par. In fact, you shoot a quadruple bogey. On the next hole you slice the ball as it falls off the tee and want to allow yourself a mulligan. But your partner's a stickler for rules. Even your caddie thinks you're a hacker and that you should be assessed a penalty for even asking.

So what are we talking about here? Why, the basics of golf, and if you need a translation, you'd better learn the following once and for all (to learn some other terms helpful in selecting equipment, see chapter 7; for different kinds of golf games, see chapter 6):

Golf Glossary

ace No, not the nickname of your friend who's better than you at golf. To find out what it really means, see *hole-in-one*.

address (set-up) Where the golf course is located? Okay, that too. But the *address* also refers to the moment when a player positions his body and club in readiness to swing and play a shot.

advice Any counsel from your playing partner or caddie concerning which club to use or what procedure to take on a specific stroke.

albatross As you'll find out, we're starting a bird theme here. See *double eagle*.

all square A match tied between two opposing players or sides.

amateur A golfer who plays exclusively for the love of the game, without monetary compensation.

angle of approach The degree at which the clubhead moves toward the ball.

approach shot Any stroke aimed for the green except the *tee shot*.

apron (collar, fringe, frog hair) The grassy area surrounding the *green*, having slightly longer grass but not as long as the grass in the *rough*.

arc The trajectory of the clubhead during a swing.

away To be the farthest away from the hole during a round and therefore the next to play.

back door Slang for the rear of the hole. See also *tradesman's entrance*.

back marker The lowest-handicap golfer in a group.

back nine (back holes) The last nine holes of a round.

backspin The motion of a ball when it hits the ground, then rolls back toward the player.

backswing The part of the swing from the point when you line up the clubhead to the ball, to the point where it starts back down from the top of the arc.

baffy A term once used for the 4-wood—now obsolete.

ball That little white or orange or yellow thing that's driving you crazy. The golf ball weighs 1.62 ounces and is 1.68 inches in diameter.

ball holed A golf ball is holed when it rests completely below the surface of the hole.

ball lost A ball is lost if it can't be located within five minutes from the beginning of the search.

ball mark An indentation on the green where a ball landed.

ball marker (coin) A small round object that indicates the position of a ball when the ball is lifted.

baseball grip To hold the golf club with all ten fingers touching it.

birdie That cute warm-blooded vertebrate of the class *Aves* flying overhead. That and something more relevant to golf: the score for a hole that is one less than the *par* (or expected) score for that hole. For example, holing the ball in merely two strokes rather than the expected three strokes on a par-3 hole.

bisque   A handicap stroke offered by one player to another on a hole of the beneficiary's choosing.

blaster   See *wedge*.

blind shot   A shot hidden by an obstruction.

bogey   One stroke more than the par for that hole.

bogey train   Are you on it, too? I am. It means making bogey after bogey and never par.

boundary   The edge of the course.

brassie (brassy)   An old-fashioned club equivalent to a 2-wood.

buggy   A golf cart.

bumping the ball   Moving the ball to get a better lie—this is cheating.

bunker (trap, sandtrap)   Golf can be like war, so this term fits. An intentionally maintained depression on a golf course filled with sand or sometimes grass. A bunker is one example of a *hazard*. A slang term for bunkers (sand traps) is *the beach*.

bye   When a player has no opponent in a match.

caddie (caddy)   The person who carries the golfer's bag of clubs during a round of golf and who sometimes gives advice to the golfer relating to club selection or strategy.

caddie cart   A cart for transporting clubs.

card   See *score card*.

carry   The distance a ball travels from where it is hit by a club to where it hits the ground.

casual water   Any water on a course other than a hazard, such as a puddle.

chip (chip shot)   A low, short shot, usually within 40 yards of the green. It's called a chip-in when you hole it.

chipper   A club used for chipping—typically with the loft of a 7-iron, but balanced like a putter.

chunking (hitting fat)   Taking a big *divot*. A chunk is also called a chili-dip.

cleats   The spikes on golf shoes.

cleet   A term once used for the 1-iron and 4-wood—now obsolete.

club   An instrument with a head attached to a shaft, used for hitting a golf ball.

clubface   The part of the club's head that strikes the ball—the lofted and grooved area.

clubhead (head)   The end of the club.

clubhouse   A hangout for golfers where there is eating, drinking, and discussion of the day's game.

coin   See *ball marker*.

committee   The people who oversee a competitive event.

competitor   A player in stroke play.

concede   Surrender a match.

course   The complete play area.

cross-handed   A grip with the left hand below the right (if right-handed).

cup   A term for the *hole*.

cut-up shot   A shot intended to curve the ball from left to right.

dance floor   Slang for the *green*.

dawn patrol   Pros on the bottom of a tournament scoreboard—so-called because they have to tee off first thing in the morning.

deuce   A score of two on a hole.

dimples   The indentations on the outside of a golf ball.

divot   A clump of turf sliced out when striking a ball.

dogleg   A term applied to a sharply angled *fairway*, or the hole where there is such a fairway.

dormie   When a player is ahead of the competition by the same number of holes left in the match.

double bogey   A hole score that is two strokes more than the par for that hole. See also *bogey*.

double eagle (albatross)   A hole shot that is three strokes less than the par score. See also *eagle*.

downswing   The point of the swing from the top of the arc to the striking of the ball.

draw   See *hook*.

drive   The first shot from the tee, the farthest distance from the hole. (The term is not used on par-3 holes for golfers with distance.)

driver   A golf club on which the angle of the clubface is limited in order to give tee shots maximum distance.

drive the green   Reach the green on a tee shot.

driving range   A place where one can practice hitting the ball, typically with distances marked off.

drop   A ball is dropped with an arm extended at shoulder height, when the previous ball has been lost or is unplayable.

duck hook   A shot curving far to the left.

duff   To mishit the ball, especially by striking the ground behind the ball first.

duffer   An incompetent golfer.

eagle   A hole score two less than the par score.

equity   A system for dealing with disputes that are not covered in the rule book.

etiquette   The code of sportsmanship and manners while playing.

explosion shot   Hitting the sand when trying to strike a ball out of a sand trap.

fade   See *slice*.

fairway The short-grass area on a golf course, running from the tee to the green.

fat shot Striking the earth behind the ball rather than making clean contact.

featherie An early type of golf ball made by stuffing boiled feathers inside a leather covering—now a rare collectible.

flagstick (flag, pin) The flagged pole at the hole, which makes the hole's location visible from a distance.

flat swing A near-horizontal swing.

flier A shot with no backspin—like a knuckleball in baseball—resulting from grass between clubface and ball.

fluff To mishit the ball.

follow-through The part of the swing from striking the ball to completion of motion.

foozle To make a mess of a shot.

fore A danger call to warn people of an approaching golf ball.

forecaddie Someone who is in the *rough* to mark where errant drives stop.

forward press A type of *waggle* in which the player moves the hands forward or bends the right knee before the backswing.

foursome Four golfers in play. See also *mixed foursome.*

free drop A *drop* made without a penalty stroke.

fried-egg lie A ball half-buried in sand. (The ball looks like a fried egg.)

front nine The first nine holes of a round of golf.

gallery Spectators at a golf match.

getting up and down When a player chips onto the green with one stroke and sinks a putt with one more.

gimme A short putt that a golfer is not required to make, on the assumption that it can be made easily.

golf A game that consists of using clubheads mounted on narrow shafts to strike a small, resilient ball into a series of (nine or eighteen) holes, situated at varying distances on an outdoor course with natural or artificial obstacles, or hazards, irregularly placed. The object is to put the ball into each hole in as few strokes as possible—but you knew that.

Grand Slam A term used in 1930 to describe Bobby Jones's winning the Opens and the national amateur championships in both the United States and Britain. Today the term refers to winning the British Open, the U.S. Open, the Masters, and the PGA Championship in the same year.

grass grain The direction grass grows, affecting the way a ball rolls on grass.

green The very short grass where putting occurs. "Through the green," however, is the phrase applied in the Rules of Golf to the *fairway*.

greens fee The cost of a round of golf.

grip The placement of hands on the club prior to the swing; or the leather, rubber, or cord on the part of the club that is grasped.

grounding the club Placing the base of the club on the ground surface behind the ball while *addressing* the ball. This is not permitted in a *bunker*.

ground under repair A section of turf of inferior quality or an area that is somehow damaged that has been officially marked.

gutta-percha A material similar to rubber tapped from various species of tropical trees, once used to make golf balls.

guttie (gutty) A golf ball made from *gutta-percha*.

hacker A lousy golfer—like a *duffer*. In my opinion, the problem for a hacker is in the swing, and for a duffer it's the state of mind.

half (halved)   A tied hole.

handicap   A method of equalizing competition between good and poor players. An *individual handicap* is a rating of your average score as compared to par and course rating. A *hole handicap* is the rating of the difficulty of each hole—one through nine on a nine-hole course and one through eighteen on an eighteen-hole course.

hanging lie   A ball on a steep slope.

having the honor   The golfer who scored the lowest on the previous hole has the honor of being allowed to tee off first. With follow-up shots, the person farthest from the hole has the honor.

hazard   A *bunker* (*sand trap*) or a body of water (water hazard) on or adjoining the course—a water hazard might be a creek, pond, lake, or ocean. This is not to be confused with *casual water,* which refers to a temporary puddling of water that rests above ground level or surfaces where a player steps.

head   See *clubhead.*

high-handicapper   Someone with a weak game.

hitting fat   See *chunking.*

hitting thin   Not taking any grass on a shot, causing the ball to be a line drive without the proper arc to find the target.

hockey stick   Slang for taking seven strokes to hole out (since the number 7 looks like a hockey stick).

hole (cup)   A 4-inch-wide and 4.2-inch-deep opening on the green, at which the ball is aimed.

hole-in-one (ace)   A hole-in-one occurs when a golfer hits the ball into the hole in a single stroke, the *tee shot*. The odds of achieving this feat are roughly 8,606 to 1.

holing out   Hitting the ball into the hole. Also called "putting out," if a putt is the final stroke taken.

home green   The *green* on a course's eighteenth hole.

hook (draw)   A shot curving from right to left.

horseshoe   Slang for a putt in which the ball moves around the edge of the hole, then comes back toward the golfer.

hosel   A socket in the clubhead into which the shaft is inserted.

impact   The exact moment, during a swing, when clubface meets ball.

in play   Within the boundaries of a course—the opposite of *out-of-bounds*.

intended line   An imaginary line extending from the ball to its intended destination.

in the leather   A ball that is a very short distance from the hole.

irons   Golf clubs with metal heads and faces. The loft (angle of the clubface) varies from iron to iron, which affects trajectory and distance. Irons are numbered from 1 to 9. The lower the number, the farther the ball goes.

jigger   An old-fashioned club comparable to a 4-iron.

jungle   A slang term for a *fairway* with heavy foliage.

lag   A putt that is made intentionally short of the hole, to avoid overshooting.

lateral shot   See *shank*.

lay-up   A shot played conservatively in order to avoid possible trouble.

lie   Where or how securely a ball sits on the turf.

lift   Picking up the ball before a *drop* or to clean it or mark it.

links   A term for a golf course (especially one bordering the sea).

lip out (rim the cup, cellophane bridge)   When the ball rolls along the rim of the hole but comes back out.

Little Slam   Winning the U.S. and British Amateur titles in the same year.

local rules   Special rules unique to a particular golf course.

loft   The degree that a clubface angles upward.

long irons   The 1-, 2-, and 3-*irons*.

loose impediments   Natural objects that are not attached to the earth, such as leaves, twigs, and stones.

low-handicapper   A very good player.

mark   To indicate the location of the ball, usually on the green.

mashie   An old-fashioned club comparable to a 5-iron.

mashie-iron   An old-fashioned club comparable to a 4-iron.

mashie-niblick   An old-fashioned club comparable to a 6- or 7-iron.

match play   Person against person or team against team in a nine- or eighteen-hole game, winner determined by the most holes won.

metal wood   "Wood" club (2-, 3-, or 4-driver) made of metal.

middle irons   The 4-, 5-, and 6-*irons*.

military golf   Slang for a poor round of golf, as in the orders of a drill sergeant: "Left-right-left-right."

miniature golf   A putting game on specially built tiny courses that first became popular in the 1930s.

mixed foursome   Two men and two women competing.

mulligan   Granting a player the right to start over again if he or she is dissatisfied with the first tee shot. A mulligan is not permitted according to the rules of the game.

nap   Grass growing at an angle.

niblick   An old-fashioned club comparable to a 9-iron.

nineteenth hole   A term used to refer to the clubhouse bar.

observer   An official who advises on rulings.

obstructions   Artificial entities such as roads and paths.

open   A tournament where both amateurs and professionals may compete.

order of play   The order in which individuals compete off the first tee.

out-of-bounds (O.B.)   An area of the course that is not allowed for play, typically marked by a fence or white stakes—the opposite of *in play*.

outside agency   Anything not belonging to the competitor, such as a *forecaddie, marker,* or *observer.*

par (ground score)   What the beginner is aiming for and what the pro tries to avoid. Par is the number of strokes a competent player would be expected to play on a particular hole. A golf course is divided into eighteen holes representing a mixture of par-3s, par-4s, and par-5s. For example, a par-4 hole should be completed in two full swings and two putts— a total of four strokes.

partner   A player with whom you win or lose, in competition with opponents.

penalty (penalty stroke)   A stroke added to the score because of a violation of golf rules.

pick, clean, and place day   A day on a course when, because of rain and mud, one is allowed to pick up and clean the ball before shots.

pin sheet   A map given out by golf courses, showing the location of holes.

pitch   A short, high approach shot.

pitch and putt   A type of golf played on a shortened course.

pitcher   An obsolete term for a light iron club with a broad face.

pitching-niblick   An old-fashioned club comparable to an 8-iron.

playing it down   Playing the ball where it lies.

play-off   The use of additional holes for settling a tie.

play through   Permitting a faster group to play a hole before a slower group.

point of nearest relief   A point no more than one club length away, but no closer to the hole, where you are allowed to drop the ball if it should land in an area of *ground under repair* or *casual water*.

practice green   A place for practicing putting.

preferred lies   A temporary rule allowing players to move the balls to better locations because of wet conditions on the course.

press   A type of bet in a nontournament game—a bet initiated in *match play* for remaining holes by the party that has already lost the entire match.

private club   A golf club where only members and guests can play. A semiprivate club has members, but is open to the public.

pro-am   A tournament in which professionals and amateurs (often celebrities) team up.

professional   A golfer who plays for money.

pro side   The higher side of the hole on an incline.

provisional ball   A second ball used to replace a lost ball until it is certain the first ball is in fact lost.

public course   A golf course open to the general public.

pull cart   A nonmotorized cart to transport a bag of clubs.

pulling the pin   Taking the flagstick out of the hole for putting.

putt   A single stroke on the *green.*

putter   A straight-faced club used on the putting *green.*

quadruple bogey   A hole score that is four strokes above par for that hole.

quail high   A term used to describe a ball hit low.

rabbit   A novice golfer.

reading the green   Studying the path of the ball to the hole and the grass grain.

recovery shot   Striking the ball out of a trouble spot.

rough   Any area of tall grass bordering the *fairway* or surrounding the *green.*

round   Nine or eighteen holes of golf, depending on the course.

rub of the green   Any odd occurrence in a game, such as the accidental deflection of a ball in flight.

Rules of Golf   The official rules of the game as determined by the Royal and Ancient Golf Club of St. Andrews and the United States Golf Association.

sandie   A type of bet in a nontournament game—a bonus bet for par out of the sand.

sand iron   A club used for *bunker* shots.

sand trap   See *bunker.*

scorecard (card)   The form where you write down your golfing score.

scratch player   A player who averages par.

scratch score   True par—a term formerly used by the Standard Scratch and Handicapping Scheme of the Council of National Golf Unions.

senior   A professional golfer at age fifty or an amateur at age fifty-five.

shag   To retrieve balls used for practice.

shank (lateral shot)   A shot in which the ball strikes the *hosel* on the inside of the clubface, causing the ball to shoot out at almost a right angle.

short game   Chipping and putting.

short irons   The 7-, 8-, and 9-*irons*; also called *wedges*.

sink   To hole a putt.

sky   A high but short shot.

slice (fade, banana ball, cut shot)   A shot curving from left to right.

slope   A course handicap, figured differently from the USGA handicap. It appears on the scorecard or is posted in the clubhouse.

smile   Slang for a cut in the ball from a mishit.

snake   A type of bet in a nontournament game—the last person to three-putt pays up; also, a long putt.

spade-mashie   An old-fashioned club comparable to a 6-iron.

spoons   An early term for certain woods because they were designed with concave faces resembling spoons.

square   When feet are parallel to the target line in a *stance*.

stance   The placing of the feet when getting ready to hit the ball.

stroke   The act of hitting the ball.

stroke hole   Hole where a stoke is given or received, based on handicapping.

stymie   When an obstacle, such as a tree, rock, or ridge, blocks the target area.

sucker pin   Slang for a hole situated near a hazard.

sucker's side   Slang for the lower side of the hole on an incline (where suckers aim).

summer rules (summer golf)   Playing the ball where it lies as in tournament golf; as opposed to *winter rules*.

sweet spot   The center of the clubface where you want to hit the ball.

swing plane   The angle at which the club travels around the body during a swing.

swing speed   The measurement in miles per hour of the speed of a swing at the point of impact.

takeaway   The beginning of a *backswing.*

target   The place the golfer intends the ball to land.

tee   A peg traditionally made of wood (plastic, metal, and biodegradable materials also are used) that holds the ball one-half inch off the ground for hitting the first drive on each hole. Most golfers use the traditional wooden tee, painted white.

tee box   The location where you place your tee to begin playing a hole.

teeing ground   An area at the start of every hole from which you drive your first shot.

teeing off   Taking a shot from the teeing ground (starting a hole).

tee shot   A shot from the teeing ground.

tempo   The rhythm of the swing.

Texas wedge   The term, popularized by Ben Hogan, for a putter used instead of a *chipper* to get the ball onto the green. A putter is used because windy conditions in Texas make keeping the ball low advantageous.

threeball   A game in which three golfers compete.

tiger   A slang term for an expert golfer.

tiger tees   The back tees or blue tees, where better golfers tee off.

tradesman's entrance   The back or side of a hole in reference to a shot.

trap   See *bunker.*

triple bogey   A hole score that is three strokes more than the par score for that hole.

unplayable lie   When it is impossible to advance the ball with a swing because of ground conditions or an obstruction.

upright swing   A swing with a steep plane.

Vardon grip   An overlapping grip of the club, popularized by Harry Vardon.

waggle   Slight movement of hands (and possibly knees) at *address* to lessen tension.

wedge   A type of *short iron*, with a lofted clubhead, used for *pitch* shots.

whiff (airball)   Missing a ball completely with a swing.

whipping   A twine binding formerly used to reinforce the joint of a club where the shaft meets the head; nowadays other materials are used for reinforcement.

wiggle   A movement of the hips before addressing the ball, to lessen tension and prepare for a shot.

winter rules   Allowing the moving of a ball to get a better lie when course conditions are poor, i.e., *preferred lies*, as opposed to *summer rules.*

woods   One place to avoid hitting the ball. More to the point, golf clubs used to hit the ball the farthest distance. Modern "woods" often are made of metal.

worm burner   Slang for a shot that rolls over the grass so fast that the worms better duck.

worthy   An early Scottish term for a player of golf.

x'd out ball   An imperfect ball sold cheaply.

yips (yippies)   A nervous twitching of the hands—usually used in reference to putting (but I get them when driving, too).

Ben Crenshaw (*Layne Murdoch*)

Zen Golf. What's that? Golf is compared to the practice of Zen more than other sports because there is time to think before the active parts of the game and because you have to control your inner self to such a degree. In other sports, the ball moves and actions are reactive. A meditative approach is in order if you want to control the yips.

Etymology of Key Golfing Words

Now that you know what all those golf terms mean, let's explore how some of the more colorful ones came to be. By the way, the name of the game we love so much is derived from the German word *kolbe*, meaning "club," via late Middle English *colf* or *colve*.

birdie The term *birdie*, or a score of one under par on a hole, came into use in 1903. An Atlantic City native by the name of A. H. Smith reportedly remarked upon holing out: "That's a bird of a shot!" Out of this avian reference, the terms *eagle* and *double eagle* soon took flight as well.

bogey Yes, it does come from the phrase *bogey man*. One fine nineteenth-century day at the Great Yarmouth Club in England, a Major Charles Wellman reportedly referred to his failure to achieve par as "getting caught by the bogey man." In regard to poor play, club members began speaking of a Colonel Bogey who always shot par. In the United States the term evolved to indicate one over par on a hole.

bunker The word *bunker*, which is another way to say "sand trap," is derived from the Scottish word *bonker* in reference to a box or a chest for storing coal, typically dug into the side of a hill. When cows grazed in the marshlands lining the early Scottish courses, they created depressions that reminded the players of the *bonkers*.

caddie (caddy) The term *caddie* is thought to be derived from *cadet*, originally a French word meaning "young man." The Scottish originally applied it to porters and other helpers, but it became a golfing term as well because Mary, Queen of Scots, had the young men of her court carry her clubs and perform other tasks on the golf course.

divot A divot, though something to avoid, is pleasant sounding—the Scottish word refers to a piece of turf.

dormie If you're ahead by the same number of holes remaining in a match, that's a dormie. The root word is Latin for "sleep" as in the French *dormir* ("to sleep")—you'd have to fall asleep to lose.

fairway Fairway evolved out of the term *fair green*, as opposed to the *rough*.

fore Etymology is often just a best guess. In the case of the term *fore* the best guess for its derivation is the British military. Before they fired a volley, artillery forces would yell "Beware before!" to warn the advancing infantry to lie down to avoid being struck by friendly fire.

gallery The term *gallery* in reference to spectators originated in England, where the balconies in theaters are known by that name.

links This term for a golf course comes from the Old English for "rising ground." *Linksland* is a word applied to dunes that are found along the seashore. Originally a links golf course referred to one found along a seashore, but now it is used for all courses.

mulligan   I've defined *mulligan* above, so you know the term refers to a second chance at teeing off. But why? No one knows where it came from. One theory: The last two syllables rhyme with "again." So "mull over it again" or "have at it again."

pro side   The higher side of the hole on an incline is called the pro side because good players read the break of a putt to target it. The low side of the hole on an incline is therefore the sucker's side.

putt   The derivation of the golf term *putt* is as simple as it seems. Just drop the final *t* and "put" the ball in the hole.

round   The term *round* applied to golf comes from the fact that early golf courses were designed to be circular—starting at the clubhouse and circling back there by the last hole.

rub of the green   You've heard the phrase "there's the rub," meaning something akin to "that's the problem" or "there's the bad luck." So *rub of the green* has nothing to do with friction. In 1812 the Royal and Ancient Golf Committee established the following rule: "Whatever happens to a ball by accident must be reckoned a rub of the green."

skins   We've all heard about those "skins" competitions and we've caught on that they have nothing to do with football and pigskin. Then what? Well, you remember that once upon a time pelts, or animal *skins*, were a medium of exchange. Hunters proudly displayed and traded their skins. So in golf the term is interchangeable with *money* or *dollars* or even *yen*.

stymie   The term *stymie* refers to the blocking of the path to the hole by an obstacle such as a tree. The Scottish word *styme* refers to a partially blind person. In earlier golf rules, a player could use his ball to block his opponent's line to the hole. The player could not "see" the hole properly, thus he was "stymied."

tee   Once again the Scottish connection. *Tee* is thought to come from the Scottish word *teay*, referring to a small pile of sand. Early golfers used piles of sand or dirt to hold the ball for driving. The wooden tee was designed by a certain Dr. William Lowell, a dentist from Boston, in 1920.

And what's the origin of *duffer*, a colorful word bandied about? I'm sorry to say that it's etymology is unknown.

7

Law and Order
(Rules and Etiquette)

I think most of the rules of golf stink. They were written by guys who can't even break a hundred.
—CHI CHI RODRIGUEZ

The first thing any beginning golfer should learn is the code of etiquette.
—EDWARD F. CHUI (chairman of the Physical Education Department at the University of Miami)

This chapter offers a bottom-line summary of golf rules and etiquette. Don't embarrass yourself. Learn them.

Law: Basic Rules

The Rules of Golf are determined by two organizations: The Royal and Ancient Golf Club of St. Andrews (R&A) and the United States Golf Association (USGA). These two organizations meet every four years (at "quadrennial conferences") to review the rules and any new equipment. Anyone serious about golf should purchase a copy of the *Official USGA Rules of Golf* and its companion volume, *Decisions on the Rules of Golf*. Here are some basic rules to get you familiar with the terrain—both geographical and psychological.

Warning!—Penalty Defined

A penalty is a stroke added to the score because of a violation of the rules. It's not quite as bad as jail, but when a game's on the line, you'd probably opt for jail.

The Magic Number—How Many Clubs?

Tournament players are allowed to carry no more than fourteen USGA-approved clubs in the golf bag. If you need more than that, take up a new sport. There are no other restrictions on the gear carried (a baseball glove to catch errant balls?).

Not to Belabor the Obvious, but . . .

You are responsible for playing your own ball—put a mark on it in case someone else has the same brand and number. You have to hole out each hole and you have to play the ball as it lies.

No Spitballs

You are not allowed to put any foreign substance on the ball that might change its flight.

No Binoculars, Telescopes, Range-Finders, Surveyor's Levels, Quadrants, Sextants, or the Like

Other than glasses and contacts, no artificial devices are allowed to enhance your vision or measuring ability.

Tee Time

You have to tee off from within the tee markers on the teeing ground and no more than two club lengths behind them. There is no penalty for a ball dropping off a tee before the swing (other than embarrassment). If the wind blows it off while you're swinging, though, it counts as a stroke and reteeing is not permitted. (In reality, in friendly games, as often as not a mulligan will be allowed in such an event.)

Par and Distance: Par is assigned to a hole based on the length of the hole and the terrain. The guidelines applied by the USGA regarding distance are as follows. For men, up to 250 yards, par 3; 251 to 470 yards, par 4; and more than 470 yards, par 5. For women, up to 210 yards, par 3; 211 to 400 yards, par 4; and 401 to 575 yards, par 5.

Proper Order

You're not allowed to play out of turn. You might do this to give a friend an advantage if you're out of contention and he's not—so that he might see how a particular club worked and how the ball traveled.

Unplayable but Not Terminal

If a ball is in an unplayable lie, such as up against a wall or buried in sand or in the middle of a bush, you can hit it from the original spot, drop it within two club lengths of its lie (but no closer to the hole), or walk away from the lie (and the hole) on a line drawn between the lie and the hole and drop the ball. Add a penalty stoke for any of the above.

Lost but Not Forgotten—Ball Lost

A ball is considered lost if it can't be located within five minutes from the beginning of the search. If it is indeed lost, you count the first stroke, add a penalty stroke, and hit a ball from the first ball's point of origin.

No Mercy—Out-of-Bounds

Out-of-bounds areas—adjoining areas not allowed for play—are usually marked with a fence or white stakes. If you hit the ball out-of-bounds, you count that stroke, add another stroke as the penalty, then hit a new ball from where you hit the first and count that stroke too. You have just "lost stroke and distance." (If you're not certain the ball has gone out-of-bounds—it's often hard to tell—you announce that you're going to hit a "provisional ball." If, on proceeding down the fairway, you discover that the first ball was not out-of-bounds after all, you pick up the provisional ball and play the original ball without penalty. This is not as great as it sounds because sometimes you'd prefer the second lie and the additional stroke.)

Relief Is Just a Drop Away—Ground Under Repair and Casual Water

You are allowed to pick up your ball and drop it no more than a club length away, but no closer to the hole—the "point of nearest relief"—if you hit the ball into an area marked "ground under repair" or an area of casual water (a puddle). No penalty is assessed. How liberal!

Hazardous to Your Game—Sand Traps

When hitting the ball out of a bunker (sand trap), you're not allowed to "ground the club" while addressing the ball—that is to say, you cannot touch the sand with the clubhead prior to your shot. Let's not forget, you have to pay for your mistakes. And you might cause those particles of sand to slip and slide and move the ball. The only legal way to test the sand's consistency is to work your feet into the sand (which is the favored technique since it helps prevent slipping during the swing). You're not even allowed to test a nearby hazard with similar consistency.

Even More Hazardous to Your Game—Water Hazards

There are two kinds of water hazards: regular, marked on the course by yellow stakes; and lateral, marked on the course by red stakes.

First, the regular: If you hit into or next to the water, you can either: (1) if possible, play it from where it lies with no penalty; or (2) drop the ball on an imaginary line between the original shot and point of entry over the water or anywhere on an imaginary line between the hole and the point of entry (but not closer to the hole than the point of entry), adding a penalty stroke; or (3) play from where you played the original shot, adding a stroke (therefore losing both stroke and distance).

Now, the lateral: If you hit into or next to the water, you have the above three options plus (4) drop the ball within two club lengths from the point of entry over the water, but no closer to the hole, adding a penalty; or (5) drop a ball in a spot across the water from the point of entry two club lengths from the hazard, but no closer to the hole, adding a penalty.

The Lodge at Pebble Beach (*Pebble Beach Company*)

Pathways and the Lie

If your ball lands on a golf cart path, you have two no-penalty options: (1) play the ball where it lies, or (2) find the point of nearest relief (where the path ends) and drop your ball one club length away from that point, but no closer to the hole.

No Landscaping, Please

You're not allowed to "build a stance," which refers to altering the surface of the earth or standing on an object to make your stance level if your lie is a difficult one.

How do you properly drop a golf ball for relief? Hold it at arm's length at a right angle to your body and let go. It used to be that you had to drop it over your shoulder, but too often the ball bounced off the shoulder or the foot, so the rule was modified.

A Sampling of Golf Games

Stroke Play (Medal Play)

Stroke play is your basic golf game. You count each stroke during a round of nine or eighteen holes and add them up. The lowest score wins.

Match Play

In match play you count each stroke for each hole. The player who has the fewest strokes wins that hole. Whoever wins the most holes wins the match.

Nassau

A match played by keeping track of the scores on the front nine, the back nine, and for the total eighteen. With regard to betting during the game of Nassau, a player or side can double the amount of a bet (a "press") for the rest of the match if down by two holes—a type of match and betting popularized in the Caribbean Islands.

Skins

A match, typically played with four people, in which each hole is a game unto itself—the winner of each hole gets a "skin." In the case of a tie, no one wins the skin. A skin can be carried over to the subsequent hole, making it worth twice as much.

Four Ball

Four Ball (sometimes called Best Ball—see below) is played by teams of two to four players. After each hole, the individual's best score on a hole becomes the team's score for that hole. The team with the lowest score at the end of the round wins.

Best Ball

In Best Ball (a name also used for Four Ball), one player goes against the better ball of two or three players.

Scramble

Scramble is played by teams of two to four players. Everyone tees off. Each team decides which of its members has the best lie and everyone shoots from there. The team with the lowest combined score at the end of the round wins.

The Handicap

If using handicaps, they're counted by adding up one's strokes after a round then subtracting the individual handicap to determine a net score.

Order: Basic Etiquette

Don't Be Late and Tee on Time

It's a cardinal sin to be late for tee time. And don't dawdle from then on—be ready to hit the ball when it's your turn.

No Crowding, Please

Give people space when they're hitting the ball. And don't fidget.

Silence is Golden

Be considerate of other people's right to silence when they're shooting.

Look Before You Strike

Make certain everyone in front of you is well out of danger of being hit by a ball before you swing.

Ample Warning

There's one time to make a lot of noise on the golf course. Don't forget to yell, "Fore!" to warn people that a golf ball is heading their way. And don't dare yell it for any other reason.

Out of the Way, You

It is considered improper to walk across someone's line before a putt because of possible changes to the ground and because it can affect a player's visualization and concentration.

For Professionals Only

Watch your language. A foul temper is reserved for name golfers. (Hey, they've earned their right for some latitude—the rest of us are just chumps if we curse and throw clubs.)

Slowpokes Should Be Nice Folks

If the group behind you is speedier or smaller than your own, let them play through. You'll find it a lot more relaxing not to have someone hurrying you.

Golfers and Gardeners

It's considered proper etiquette to replace divots. Put them back where they came from and step on them to help the grass's chance of rooting again. Some courses will even give you a bag of dirt and sand along with grass seed to patch any holes you create. Along these same lines, rake the bunkers if you wreak havoc with them (and don't enter them by walking down the face—enter from the back). And repair ball marks on the greens (but not spike marks, which the Rules of Golf forbid doing in order to prevent a player from forming a depression or series of them that might affect a putt).

Impressionable

Do not take your golf bag onto the green because it might leave a mark—and no jumping up and down for joy.

Flag Duty

The last person to putt tends the flag until someone holes out, whereupon that person takes over flag duty and eventually replaces the flag before moving onto the next hole.

Scorekeepers

State the score after each hole if you're down. But if you're up and the down player fails to state the score, you should say it, in order to avoid later resentment over a disputed point.

Moving Right Along

No lingering on the green, writing down scores. Remember, there are others behind you.

Honor Bestowed

Having the honor refers to the practice of letting the player who scored the lowest on the previous hole tee off first. The advantage is that a player can swing without the pressure of knowing what his opponent has accomplished in his shot. After the tee shots, the person farthest from the hole goes first. On the green, the person farthest from the hole putts first—he can choose to hole out or let the next person farthest from the hole putt.

Gimme, Will Ya?

In a friendly game, you might want to follow the tradition that a putt is *given* (a *gimme*)—that is, assumed to be holed out—when it's less than the length of a putter's grip. A gimme putt is picked up, not struck.

8

Tools of the Trade: Golf Equipment

If you are going to throw a club, it is important
to throw it ahead of you, down the fairway, so
you don't waste energy going back to pick it up.
—Tommy Bolt

Golf equipment has evolved over the years and is a fascinating study in itself. At the present, it is big business and a high-tech pursuit, with new products appearing often. If you're serious about your golf, it pays to have a sense of where equipment's been and where it's going. And to stay competitive, it pays to update your gear every few years.

Golf Balls

A Brief History

The manufacturing of golf balls is central to the game's development. Prior to the seventeenth century, balls were wooden. Later they were made of boiled feathers (mostly chicken feathers) compressed inside a leather covering. Special tools were required for the arduous and tedious feather-stuffing process. When the leather covering was packed to capacity, it was worked into a sphere. On drying, the feathers expanded, and the leather was painted white.

Although the feather balls could be hit a great distance, they had major drawbacks: In addition to being expensive, they were vulnerable in wet weather and tended to lose their spherical shape with continued use.

In 1848 golf balls began to be made of hardened gutta-percha, a resinous substance derived from several different species of tropical trees. Because gutta-percha balls, or gutties, were inexpensive—one-fifth the cost of feather-and-leather balls—golf became a much more affordable game to play.

During the early twentieth century, golf balls started to be made by winding a rubber thread around a core of solid rubber. Unlike the gutta-percha ball, the new ball was resilient and responsive, making it easier to play. Golf's popularity increased even more.

The Modern Ball

The modern golf ball weighs 1.62 ounces and is 1.68 inches in diameter. Golf balls nowadays are made of one, two, or three elements, of rubber or plastic. The one-piece balls are not suitable for the game—you'll get to whack them on driving ranges. Two-piece balls have a core and a cover. Three-piece balls are made of a core wrapped with strands of rubber and a cover. Two-piece balls are less expensive, wear better, and travel farther. Three-piece balls tend to spin more and offer more control for the experienced golfer.

There are two types of covers, hard and soft. A hard cover, made of Surlyn (a type of plastic) is less expensive, wears better, and travels farther. A soft cover, made of Balata (a rubberlike material), is more expensive, but offers more control. Some balls are now made with titanium cores. Titanium is a metallic element that is also used in clubs.

Balls are rated by compression, low to high—either 80 (soft), 90 (medium), or 100 (high). The faster your swing, the higher compression you should use, although some pros stick with the 90-rated ball, believing it offers more control. (Another point to factor in—when it's hot you might want to use the 100 ball because heat softens the ball.) Balls have ID numbers, 1 through 4, to help you keep track of your ball. Laundry markers do wonders in that department, too.

Golf pros change balls every few holes, because the balls tend to get out of round.

Why do golf balls have dimples (typically 382 or 384; sometimes so marked)? It's physics, the same aerodynamic principle used in the designing of airplane wings. The dimples provide lift. When the ball is hit, it spins. As the ball comes off the club, the dimples trap air in such a way that the air moves more rapidly over the top of the ball than the bottom, causing the ball to lift.

Golf Clubs

The parts of a golf club are as follows: *grip* (handle); *shaft* (between the grip and head); *head* (or *clubhead*—the weighted bottom of the club used to hit the ball); *hosel* (a socket in the head into which the shaft is inserted; *neck* (the curved part of the head next to the shaft); *heel* (the crook of the head near the shaft); *face* (or *clubface* or, in the case of irons, *blade*—the part of the head that strikes the ball); *toe* (or *nose*—the end of the head away from the shaft); *sole* (the base of the clubhead); and *flange*—the projecting piece of a clubhead behind the sole.

By the way, those clubs in the attic that belonged to your grandfather, although works of wonderful craftsmanship, are obsolete. Woods—once called brassies and baffies—are now made of metal as well as wood; and the irons—known as mashies, niblicks, and pitchers—are now made of high-tech alloys.

A new set typically has seven (a starter set) or eleven (a full set) clubs. A starter set usually has five irons, including a Number 3, 5, 7, 9, and a putter; and two woods, a Number 1 (the driver) and a 3. A full set of clubs usually has ten irons, including a 3-, 4-, 5-, 6-, 7-, 8-, and 9-iron, and a pitching wedge; and three woods, a 1 (the driver), 3, and 5.

Some golfers also carry specialty irons, such as a 1 and 2, a sand wedge, a lob wedge, a chipper, and a driving iron; or specialty woods, such as a 2, 4, 7, or 9. (In case you haven't caught on, the lower the number, the farther it's expected to carry the ball.)

When experienced players tee off, they use the driver. Beginners will have more control with the 3-wood or, on a short hole, a 3-iron. For an approach shot, there's no rule of thumb—either a wood or an iron might work better for you. When shooting out of hazards, you might want to get familiar with your specialty clubs. When chipping (shooting from within 40 yards of the green), the wedges work well. On the green, it's time for your chosen putter. (The putter, by the way, is the club that should be propped near you right now—it has a soul and a personality and gets lonely for you.)

Here are some other facts and terms you should know when purchasing clubs:

- When you pick up a golf club (ah, the feel of this precision instrument!), you'll note that the grip tapers from top to bottom (i.e., it's wider at the end of the shaft) unlike a baseball bat, which is narrower at the end. This design feature results from the fact that in a golf grip more of the palms are at the top with the fingers extending to the narrower area. Also, the physics of the swing necessitates a flexing of the shaft.
- Golf clubs are sized to each player. A pro shop can help you find the right length based on your height, the length of your arms, your address, and your swing. A matched set has clubs designed to look and feel the same.
- Grips come in different materials—leather, cord, all rubber, and half rubber—and in different thicknesses—in increments of 1/32 of an inch. The thicker grips (sometimes called jumbo grips) restrict wrist and hand action (allowing less hooking); thinner grips permit greater wrist and hand action (allowing less slicing). A putter is the only club that can have a flat grip—allowing the placement of both thumbs along the middle of the shaft for better control.
- *Static weight* is the club's overall weight. *Swing weight* is the club's weight distribution based on a point of balance between the head and the end of the grip.

- Shafts come in different *flexes*, typically: extra-stiff, stiff, regular, and soft. The more powerful your swing, the less flex you need to have additional kick.
- Until the early 1700s, all golf clubs were made of wood. At that time craftsmen began experimenting with metals for specialty clubs. By the late 1800s, irons were a standard part of a club set. Shafts for all of them were still made from wood, in particular hickory. Starting in 1929, however, steel became the shaft material of choice. For a time in the 1960s, aluminum was also used, but it proved to be too soft for proper flex and torque and lost favor. A material commonly added to shafts is graphite, a form of carbon, that is flexible but strong. The most expensive shafts now contain titanium, a metallic element with properties of lightness, flex, and torque similar to graphite. Boron is a nonmetallic element also added to shafts because it hardens steel when alloyed with it—very Space Age, both.
- Forged-iron clubs are made individually without a mold; investment-cast clubs are made from a mold.
- Beryllium copper is sometimes added to clubheads to add weight.
- The head of a *laminated wood* club is made by gluing layers of wood together. A *persimmon wood* is made from a solid piece of wood—named after trees of the ebony family that have wood hard enough for this purpose (those in the know look for matching grain patterns). Wood clubs actually made from metal are sometimes referred to as Pittsburgh Persimmon.
- Making woods from metal, by the way, allows for redistributing weight for special design purposes. In *perimeter weighting,*

for instance, there is more weight around the perimeter of the clubface to reduce the amount of twisting on striking the ball.

- Similarly, woods and irons are both sometimes referred to as cavity back. This means they have had the weight of the back of the clubhead removed—that is, hollowed out behind the hitting area—and redistributed around the perimeter of the clubhead. With more weight in the clubhead's heel and toe areas, a player tends to hit straighter shots when contact is off-center. A "muscle-back" iron has a bulge behind the clubface to add mass for power.

- A *round-soled* club is rounded from heel to toe, as opposed to a *flat-soled* club—the former is more adaptable to different slopes.

- The *bulge* is the curve across the face of a wood.

- The *lie-angle* of a club is the angle of the shaft to the clubhead. There's quite a variety.

- With a *blind-bore* club, you cannot see the end of the shaft on the head's sole. With a *through-bore* club, you can see the shaft. The latter design tends to be used in stiffer shafts.

- A *radiused* (also called *cambered* or *rocker-soled*) club has a curved sole (curved from heel to toe), the idea being to enable the golfer to avoid hitting too much ground on difficult lies or dry fairways.

- With an *offset* club, the clubface is set back from the hosel, the idea being to encourage a swing that hits down on the ball.

- On a *center-shafted* putter, the shaft is joined to the center of the clubhead. On an *end-shafted* putter, the shaft is joined closer to the end.

- By the way, you'll want to buy some headcovers for your clubs. They can be vinyl, fabric, leather, or sheepskin.

Fred Couples (*Lane Murdoch*)

Why do clubfaces have grooves? The groves on a clubface prevent the ball from sliding upward on impact.

Golf Bags

There are three basic types of golf bags: carry bags, pull-cart bags, and riding-cart bags. They go from light to heavy with increasing numbers of compartments.

Here are some variations:

- A *drainpipe carry bag* holds about six or seven clubs—good for practicing.
- A *light carry bag* is collapsible and also holds a partial set of clubs.
- A *pull-cart bag* is rigid and can be either carried or used on a pull cart. It holds a full club set, as do all of the following bags.
- A *divider bag* has compartments for each club.
- An *all-in-one bag* has additional compartments.
- A *tournament bag* is what the pros use.

With any of these bags, be sure you get a strong enough strap—the straps on cheaper bags frequently break after very little use.

If you purchase an all-in-one bag or a tournament bag, you might want to carry the following besides clubs, balls, and tees: extra gloves, extra shoes and socks, sweater or sweatshirt, umbrella and raingear (including hoods for the clubs), towel, spikes, spike wrench, rules book, yardage book, coins, pencils, first-aid kit, snakebite kit, sunscreen, water, food, and—why not?—a cellular phone. And hanging from a strap on the golf bag—a towel to clean your clubheads.

Golf Shoes and Gloves

Golf shoes should be considered equipment, even if you factor in fashion when you buy them. The spikes are arranged to maximize swing efficiency. Most golf shoes have spikes lining the outside of both the sole and heel areas, allowing the golfer to push off the rear foot on the downswing, with the front foot receiving the weight transfer without slipping forward on hitting the ball and afterward.

With gloves, we're also in the realm of equipment. A glove helps in the gripping of a club, but since one hand overlaps the other in a proper grip, only one glove is called for. (If you're right-handed, wear a glove on the left hand, and vice-versa.) The ungloved hand can better feel and control the action of the club. Golf gloves are made of leather or synthetic materials. Leather, especially the expensive Cabretta, offers a better feel. Golf pros carry extra gloves and change them about every six holes.

A Sens-O-Grip is a device used to measure the tightness of your grip—it bleeps if you grip too tightly. Here are some other golfing gizmos to help your game: the Head Freezer, a rectangular frame that attaches to your cap to measure head movement during a swing; the Perfect Swing Trainer, a large circular ring you lay your shaft against as you swing; and the Balance Board, which forces you to keep your balance or else you hit only air.

Clothing

In addition to having proper clubs and balls, I feel that to play his best golf a golfer must feel well-dressed.

—GARY PLAYER

There is definitely a look in golf clothing, but it's pretty wide-ranging. The bottom line is bright colors, which are traditional, going back to the game's origin in Scotland. The idea was to be *seen* on the golf course, for safety's sake, just as hunters dress colorfully so as not to be mistaken for an animal.

Some private clubs have dress codes. It's a general rule of thumb not to reveal too much flesh by wearing short-shorts or tank tops. Men who plan to go pro someday should know that the PGA Tour has guidelines for dress—shorts are not allowed.

Here's a clothing factoid: Knickers, a traditional golfing look, used to be called "plus fours." To the standard length of short pants four inches were added, or "plus four," so that they would blouse below the knee.

9

Bizarre Golf: Anecdotes for the Ages

Out of the mouths of America's most clean-cut
group of athletes, except perhaps bowlers, comes
a rich vein of slang that makes the hyped-up wild
men of the NFL seem bland.

—Thomas Boswell
(writer)

Golf, perhaps more than any other sport, offers us a tradition of anecdotes. Sure, bizarre things happen at baseball parks— remember the televised earthquake at Candlestick Park during the World Series? Golf, though, is the only sport with varied playing fields that have nature expressing itself abundantly, pairings of individualistic personalities with plenty of time to harass each other, and a special kind of interaction between player and spectator. Here's a sampling to make my point.

The Plain Truth or a Freudian Slip?

North Carolina is a mecca for golfers and promotes its courses for tourists. One tourism brochure put it this way: "Famous midsouth resorts include Pinehurst and Southern Pines, where it is said that there are more golf curses per square mile than anywhere else in the world."

First in Line

Tommy Bolt is famous for his temper tantrums and for throwing his golf clubs. In 1957, the day after the PGA adopted the Tommy Bolt Rule, prohibiting the throwing of clubs, Bolt jettisoned his club—not so much because he was raging at the moment, but because he wanted to be certain to be the first golfer fined under "his" rule.

A Little Too Close

Tony Lema, Gene Sarazen, and Andy Bean, among others, have all had their golf balls land in the laps of women. Technically, the golfers could have played the balls right from the laps, but all chose to drop the ball at the location of the female spectator and continue. Moral: A gentleman golfer is always a gentleman.

Bull's-Eye, Sort of

At the 1973 Sea Pines Heritage Classic in Hilton Head, South Carolina, Hale Irwin's golf ball landed inside a woman's bra—a rare example of hitting a ball between two. Although the rulebook states a golfer is supposed to retrieve the ball from an obstruction and drop it, an exception was made in this case—the "obstruction" was allowed to remove the ball herself.

Row, Row, Row the Boat

At the 1913 Shawnee (Oklahoma) Invitational for Ladies, Mrs. J. F. Meehan shot a 166 for the 130-yard sixteenth hole. Her tee shot ended up in the Binniekill River and the ball floated. With her husband rowing, she followed the ball in a boat, managing to play it a mile and a half away. Then she had a number of shots through a forest to reach the green.

The Love Letter

"Don't look for me in the gallery," the note said. Gene Sarazen received an orange tie with that message enclosed from someone he believed to be a Ziegfield showgirl. The note went on to say that the writer desperately wanted Sarazen to beat Walter Hagen at the 1922 Westchester-Biltmore. Sarazen, out of natural curiosity, kept scanning the gallery for the "showgirl" who sent the letter and lost his concentration. When Hagen complimented him on his orange tie, Sarazen figured out who had really sent him the tie and note.

The Price of Celebrity

In the 1964 U.S. Open, Gary Player signed autographs while standing in a lake. He had accidentally been pushed into the water by adoring fans.

A Greener Shade of Pale

Titanic Thompson was a known hustler on the courses from the 1920s until his death in the 1970s. In a favorite hustle, he would claim he hadn't played for months due to illness. His pale skin would seem to corroborate his claim. Still, he accepted big bets, played golf that day, and won easily. Thompson, in fact, praticed hard right up to the challenge. The reason for his lack of a tan was that, during his months of pre-bet practice, he purposely wore a big hat, long sleeves, and gloves.

Tom Kite (*Lane Murdoch*)

True Lies

In a practice round before the 1967 Masters, on the thirteenth hole of Augusta, fifty-five-year-old Sam Snead made a $5 Nassau bet (see page 95) with twenty-year-old Bobby Cole of South Africa, the 1966 British Amateur champion. Pointing to a stand of pines on the hole's dogleg, Snead challenged, "Bobby, when I was your age, I could knock the ball over those pine trees." Cole went for it, but didn't even come close to clearing the trees. He asked Snead, "How did you do it?" Snead explained, with a devilish grin, how, when he was Cole's age, the trees were thirty-five years shorter. By the way, Snead won the Nassau.

Quitting Time

At Cypress Point, on the sixteenth hole, after a drive which hit the cliff below the green fell to the beach, Henry Ransom, a pro from Texas, tried unsuccessfully to clear the cliff three shots in a row. On the fourth shot, the ball bounced off the rocks and hit him in the stomach. Ransom told his caddie to retrieve the ball and stormed off, saying, "When the hole starts hitting back at me, it's time to quit."

Told You So

Baltusrol Golf Course in Springfield, New Jersey, needed a toughening up for the 1954 U.S. Open. Course designer Robert Trent Jones got the job and set about altering several holes. He took some criticism for his work on the fourth hole for the 200-yard approach across water where three bunkers waited—a par-3. To test it, Jones played the hole with the chairman of the Open committee, the club president, and the club pro. On Jones's turn, he hit a hole-in-one and stated, "As you can see, gentlemen, this hole is not too tough."

Divot of Death

During a world tour in 1937, Walter Hagen and trick-shot golfer Joe Kirkwood played a golf course in Shanghai, China, constructed over a sacred burial ground. The corpses were not six-feet under, however, but merely laid on the surface and covered with earth, as is traditional there. On the eighteenth hole, Kirkwood's tee shot landed on a burial mound bordering the fairway. Hagen warned him not to take too much divot, but Kirkwood ignored the advice. After his shot, Kirkwood looked down to see an elbow sticking up.

Of Lost Balls and Doggy Treats

Tony Green of the Scottish international team liked to take his golden retriever Ben to the links with him. One day, after a practice round, Green became worried because Ben looked so sick, and he took the dog to a vet. The vet recommended surgery to see what was causing the swelling in Ben's stomach. On opening up the canine, the vet found eleven golf balls. Ben was thenceforth banned from the course.

Like Hailstones

At the Lakeside Course of San Francisco's Olympic Club, a big cypress tree is an effective obstruction at the eighth green. In 1977, when tree trimmers set to work on three branches, 105 golf balls rained down.

Whose Fault Is It, Anyway?

For years a sign at the Chandigarh Golf Club in India warned against "caddie-beating." The practice was a common problem when players were losing rounds.

A Sixth Sense

In 1990, amateur golfer Margaret Waldron of Jacksonville, Florida, legally blind at age seventy-four, shot two holes-in-one on the same hole at Long Point Golf Course with the same club two days in a row.

Imagine How the Tree Felt

In 1982, at the Memorial at Muirfield Village Golf Course in Dublin, Ohio, Johnny Miller hit the same tree three times on one hole. He kept thinking he could skirt a pine tree from different lies in the rough, but slammed it on his third, fourth, and fifth strokes. He ended up with a triple-bogey seven. He dropped from a likely fifth-place finish to twenty-second.

Another Tree's Revenge

At the 1990 Australian Open at Royal Melbourne, Bret Ogle used a 2-iron to hit a ball from a bunker past a tree. The ball hit the tree, bounced back, and broke Ogle's kneecap.

A Formidable Golf Course

An enterprising fellow by the name of Floyd Satterlee Rood played the entire United States as a golf course. He set out from the Pacific Ocean on September 14, 1963, and drove the 3,397.7-mile course in 114,737 strokes by October 3, 1964. The number of lost balls? A mere 3,511.

A Fast Surface

Sometimes surface conditions really help your ball roll. An Australian meteorologist was aided in a practice drive in 1962 at

Mawson Base, Antarctica, by the ice. His ball traveled 2,640 yards.

Give the Cow Some Credit

In 1981, at Mountain View Country Club, amateur Ted Barnhouse scored a hole-in-one by hitting three obstacles and a flagstick—a four-bouncer. On a par-3, 145-yard hole, he hit one too far to the right over a barbed-wire fence, hitting the forehead of a grazing cow. The ball ricocheted off the dense skull into a sprinkler head, then into a parked lawn mower, and then onto the green, rolling right for the flagstick, and bouncing into the hole.

Sorry, Honey

After the first day of the 1979 Masters, Mac McLendon jokingly told his wife that he was hitting so poorly that she had better not get out in front of him. On the drive off the first tee, he hooked his ball into the gallery and hit a spectator, knocking her down. Who? A lady in a brown coat—his wife. She survived with a bad bruise, but he didn't—he missed the cut.

10

Fore Play: Golf Jokes

Golf is the most fun you can have without taking your clothes off.

—CHI CHI RODRIGUEZ

Hang out at the links or in the clubhouse long enough and you'll hear a golf joke (or be the victim of a practical joke). Humor helps golfers relieve the tension between shots and rounds. Here's a taste.

For the Whole Family

One golfer to another: "I hate golf jokes."
Second golfer: "Why's that?"
First golfer: "Because they're always beating me."

What rule book do you consult if you play eighteen holes in eighteen shots?
    The Bible.

The golfer asked: "What wood should I use to guarantee a hole-in-one?"

What did his caddie reply?

"Your pencil."

What's the term used for playing golf with your boss?

A hazard.

Why did the Scotsman wear a black armband while playing golf?

He lost a ball.

What's the definition of a handicapped golfer?

Someone who plays golf with his boss.

Where does the Abominable Snowman play golf?

On the missing links.

What do alligators wear when they play golf?

Shirts with little humans on them.

In what vehicle does a wealthy golf assistant drive around?

A caddie-lac.

What's it called when a golf ball lands in the mouth of a barking dog?

A ball-in-ruff.

Who was the best golfer ever in North Africa?

Gene Saharazen.

What golfer sank a putt in the Atlantic Ocean in 1912?
   Titantic Thompson.

Why did the golfer have two pairs of pants?
   In case he got a hole-in-one.

What do you call a golf celebration?
   A par-tee.

What song did the golfer sing after he sold his golf vehicle to his assistant?
   "My Cart Belongs to Caddie."

What's the definition of a businessman golfer?
   Someone who talks golf at the office and business on the golf course.

What do a lousy golfer and a computer nerd have in common?
   They're both hackers.

Why is a hacker's golf game in good weather like a day at the beach?
   He lies in the sun.

What's the term for a golfer who doesn't work on his short game?
   A putz.

What's it called when you buy a set of golf clubs at list price?
   Getting shafted.

What's the best device on the market for lowering your golf score?

An eraser.

Why don't ministers play a lot of golf?
1. They're busy on Sunday.
2. They don't have the language for it.

The hacker told his friend, "I consistently shoot golf in the low 70s — until I get to the fifth hole."

The hacker told his friend, "I almost got a hole-in-one. I only missed by six shots."

Why do hackers prefer golf carts over caddies?

They don't criticize and they can't count.

What do golf and business have in common?

You drive hard to get in the green, then wind up in the hole.

What's the biggest water hazard for Lee Trevino?

The Golf of Mexico.

Golf . . . a game in which the ball doesn't lie well, the player does.

The hacker said to the caddie, "This is the hardest course I've ever played on."

The caddie replied, "But you haven't been on the course yet."

What's the definition of a chronic cheater in golf?

Someone who writes zero on his scorecard when he gets a hole-in-one.

What's the handicap for a hacker?

His drivers, his irons, and his putter.

Why is golf like a love affair?

If you don't take it seriously, it's no fun; if you do take it seriously, it breaks your heart.

Even if you can airmail a golf ball, it's hard to put the right address on it.

How do you tell who's the boss and who's the employee in a game of golf?

The employee is the one who says, "Oops!" when he gets a hole-in-one.

What's the most important shot in golf?

The next one.

What are golf's three ugliest words?

Still your shot.

What would a hacker have to shoot to win one of the Majors?

The rest of the field.

Then there was the duffer who birdied the second, sixth, and ninth holes ... while he was playing the third, fifth, and tenth holes.

Nick Price (*Layne Murdoch*)

What's the golf fanatic's favorite song?
"Home on the Range."

Then there was the golfer who was so upset with his game that he drank a whole bottle of whiskey before playing. He shot the happiest 99 of his life.

Then there was the golfer who was so annoyed with media reports that he thanked the press corps from the heart of his bottom.

What's the best advice a golf pro can give a hopeless hacker?
"Take off two weeks, then quit the game."

Some hackers hit in the woods so often they should wear orange hunting jackets.

What do slicers and condemned playgrounds have in common?
Lousy swings.

Then there was the hacker with the beautiful short game. Unfortunately, it was off the tee.

One good thing about golf . . . if you live long enough, you get to shoot your age.

What does golf have in common with the income tax?
It makes liars out of people.

What does golf have in common with religion?
1. Sunday worshippers.
2. There's a lot of prayer involved.

What should a duffer give a caddie after keeping him out on the course all day for a horrible round?
His clubs.

Why do golf coaches tell you to keep your head down when you hit the ball?
So you can't see them laughing.

Why is golf good for the soul?
You get so mad at yourself you forget to hate your enemies.

The duffer had one major flaw in his game ... he stood too close to the ball after he hit it.

What's the definition of a mulligan?
The chance to repeat a mistake right away.

How many golfers does it take to screw in a lightbulb?
Don't even ask. The golfers have better things to do. Call an electrician.

And why did the rabbit cross the road?
To find his lost golf ball, of course. (See chapter 5 if you've already forgotten what a "rabbit" is in golf.)

Name one thing more important than golf.
    Winning at golf.

For Older Family Members

Why is golf like sex?
    You can be lousy at it and still have fun.

Then there was the golf pro who was so upset that two of his balls went in the water that he jumped in and made it four.

Some golfers get so nervous, the greens don't need fertilizing for a year.

At least in golf, unlike life, the older you get, the more you score.

11

The Quotable Golfer

One way to understand the game of golf is to read what golfers and others have said about the game. The following quotes offer something for everyone: humor, instruction, history, philosophy, and inspiration.

Golf Is . . .

Golf is a good walk spoiled.—MARK TWAIN

Golf can make you crazy.—LEE TREVINO

Golf is a game whose aim is to hit a very small ball into a very small hole, with weapons singularly ill-designed for that purpose.—WINSTON CHURCHILL

Golf is the most human game of all. You have the same highs and lows—sometimes in the same round.—LEE TREVINO

If there is one thing I have learned during my years as a professional, it is that the only thing constant about golf is its inconstancy.—JACK NICKLAUS

Golf is a game you never can get too good at. You can improve, but you never can get to where you master the game.
—GAY BREWER

This is a game of misses. The guy who misses the best is going to win.—BEN HOGAN

Golf takes more mental energy, more concentration, more determination than any other sport ever invented.—ARNOLD PALMER

This game is like a horse. . . . If you take your eye off it, it'll jump back and kick your shins for you.—BYRON NELSON

When you play for fun, it's fun. But when you play golf for a living, it's a game of sorrows. You're never happy.—GARY PLAYER

Golf is not a game of great shots. It's a game of the most accurate misses.—GENE LITTLER

There is no need to tell one who has played a great deal of championship golf that it's the short game that decides the contests.—TOMMY ARMOUR

There are no absolutes in golf. Golf is such an individual game, and no two people swing alike.—KATHY WHITWORTH

Golf is the one game I know which becomes more and more difficult the longer one plays it.—BOBBY JONES

Golf is just a game, and an idiotic one at that.
—MARK CALCAVECCHIA (on failing to make the cut at a British Open)

Golf is a game where guts, stick-to-it-ness, and blind devotion will get you nothing but an ulcer.—TOMMY BOLT

Golf is a game of endless predicaments.—CHI CHI RODRIGUEZ

No one ever conquers golf.—KATHY WHITWORTH

Golf is not a fair game. It's a rude game.—FUZZY ZOELLER

Golf is deceptively simple and endlessly complicated. A child can play it well and a grown man can never master it. Any single round of it is full of unexpected triumphs and perfect shots that end in disaster. It is almost a science, yet it is a puzzle without an answer. It is gratifying and tantalizing, precise and unpredictable; it requires complete concentration and total relaxation. It satisfies the soul and frustrates the intellect. It is at the same time rewarding and maddening—and it is without doubt the greatest game mankind has ever invented.
—ARNOLD PALMER

Golf is so popular simply because it is the best game in the world in which to be bad.—A. A. MILNE

Golf is 20 percent mechanics and technique. The other 80 percent is philosophy, humor, tragedy, romance, melodrama, companionship, camaraderie, cussedness, and conversation.
—GRANTLAND RICE (sportswriter)

Golf is 20 percent talent and 80 percent management.
—BEN HOGAN

I'm in love with golf and I want everybody else to share my love affair.—ARNOLD PALMER

What other people may find in poetry or in art museums, I find in the flight of a good drive—the white ball sailing up and up into that blue sky, growing smaller and smaller, almost taking off in orbit, then suddenly reaching its apex, curving downward, falling, describing the perfect parabola of a good hit, and finally dropping to the turf to roll some more, the way I planned it.—ARNOLD PALMER

You are what you think you are—in golf and in life.
—RAYMOND FLOYD

The perfect round of golf has never been played. It's eighteen holes-in-one. I almost dreamt it once, but I lipped out at eighteen. I was mad as hell.—BEN HOGAN

In golf, as in life, you get out of it what you put into it.
—SAM SNEAD

Golf is a game that creates emotions that sometimes cannot be sustained with a club in the hand.—BOBBY JONES

When I play my best golf, I feel as if I'm in a fog, standing back watching the earth in orbit with a golf club in my hands.
—MICKEY WRIGHT

One minute it's fear and loathing, but hit a couple of good shots and you're on top of the world. I've gone crazy over this game.—JACK NICHOLSON

On the golf course as nowhere else, the tyranny of causality is suspended, and men are free.—JOHN UPDIKE

Golf, in short, is not so much a game as it is a creed and a religion.—ARNOLD HAULTAIN (writer)

To find a man's true character, play golf with him.
—P. G. WODEHOUSE

Hitting the ball is the fun part of it, but the fewer times you hit the ball the more fun you have. Does this make any sense?
—LOU GRAHAM (writer)

Golf is the cruelest of sports. Like life, it's unfair. It's a harlot. A trollop. It leads you on. It never lives up to its promises. It's not a sport, it's bondage. An obsession. A boulevard of broken dreams. It plays with men. And runs off with the butcher.—JIM MURRAY (writer)

Technically Speaking . . .

The only way you can improve your game is by taking the bad parts of your game and changing them. It's just as if you're sinning in some way. You can't keep doing it; you just have to quit. It's the same thing in golf; quit doing the bad things.
—BYRON NELSON

Know your strengths and take advantage of them.
—GREG NORMAN

A good swing is a physical pleasure.—BEN HOGAN

Golf swings are like snowflakes: There are no two exactly alike.—Peter Jacobsen

My swing is so bad I look like a caveman killing his lunch. —Lee Trevino

Golf is an awkward set of bodily contortions designed to produce a graceful result.—Tommy Armour

There's just no way to make the hole look bigger. —Tommy Armour

If you need a par, go for a birdie, because if you don't get the birdie, you should hopefully get the par.—Nick Faldo

Forget your opponents; always play against par.—Sam Snead

Through years of experience I have found that air offers less resistance than dirt.—Jack Nicklaus

If you can afford only one lesson, tell the pro you want it on the fundamentals: the grip, the stance, and the alignment. —Nancy Lopez

Whenever I mishit a shot or notice a swing problem, I return to the basics of swing, stance, grip, and alignment. —Kathy Whitworth

Is there such a thing as a technically perfect swing? If there is, I have yet to see it.—David Leadbetter

Ben Hogan

The ideal build for a golfer would be strong hands, big fore-arms, thin neck, big thighs, and a flat chest. He'd look like Popeye.—GARY PLAYER

When you talk turkey with a businessman, you must look squarely at him during the entire conversation. It's the same in putting.—GENE SARAZEN

Develop a consistent preshot routine.—TOM WATSON

The most important thing in golf is to have the same swing every time.—GARY PLAYER

Try to think of your golf swing as an efficient machine.
—JULIUS BOROS

Foot action is one of the main differences between a good golfer and a duffer.—SAM SNEAD

The basic factor in all good golf is the grip. Get it right, and all other progress follows.—TOMMY ARMOUR

I regard keeping the head very steady, if not absolutely stock still, throughout the swing as *the* bedrock fundamental of golf.—JACK NICKLAUS

You cannot correct a fault with a fault. That is why I do not talk about theories, but about fundamentals, and why I always go back to fundamentals.—KEN VENTURI

A good player corrects his game by being conscious of his swing. A poor player remains a poor player because he is conscious only of the ball.—KEN VENTURI

Strategizing in golf is about seizing every advantage within the rules and etiquette of the game.—JACK NICKLAUS

Trust your muscles and hit the ball to the hole. Keep it simple.
—HARVEY PENICK

Long ago I learned that no putt is short enough to take for granted.—BOBBY JONES

Treat each putt as a separate little task without worrying about what has gone before or what will come after.—BERNHARD LANGER

Study the green as you approach it.—TOM WATSON

The cardinal principle of all golf shot-making is that if you move your head, you ruin body action.—TOMMY ARMOUR

You can tell a good putt by the noise it makes.—BOBBY LOCKE

The width of the stance is really the foundation of a good swing.—GREG NORMAN

The harder I practice, the luckier I get.—GARY PLAYER

You must work very hard to become a natural golfer.
—GARY PLAYER

Practice puts your brains in your muscles.—Sam Snead

I never hit a shot, even in practice, without having a very sharp, in-focus picture of it in my head. It's like a color movie.
—Jack Nicklaus

There is nothing in this game of golf that can't be improved upon—if you practice.—Patty Berg

Undirected practice is worse than no practice. Too often you become careless and sloppy in your swing. You'd be better off staying home and beating the rugs.—Gary Player

Every day you don't hit balls is one day longer it takes you to get better.—Ben Hogan

We work on putting as much as we do the full swing—after all, if putting is half the game, it deserves half your practice time.
—Tom Watson

Practice, which some regard as a chore, should be approached as just about the most pleasant recreation ever devised.
—Babe Didrikson Zaharias

Practice until you don't have to think.—Calvin Peete

Cultivate a smooth waggle for, as the old Scotch saying goes, "As ye waggle so shall ye swing."—Tommy Armour

I'm a great believer in the benefits of a balanced, poised finish.
—Ernie Els

Golf is meant to be fun.—JACK NICKLAUS

Visualize winning.—GARY PLAYER

I say this without any reservations whatsoever: It is impossible to outplay an opponent you can't outthink.—LAWSON LITTLE

A strong mind is one of the key components that separate the great from the good.—GARY PLAYER

Action before thought is the ruination of most of your shots.
—TOMMY ARMOUR

Staying in the present is the key to any golfer's game: Once you start thinking about a shot you just messed up or what you have to do on the next nine to catch somebody, you're lost.
—PAUL AZINGER

Play with a controlled mad.—SAM SNEAD

To play well on the final holes of a major championship, you need a certain arrogance. You have to find a trance, some kind of self-hypnosis that's almost a state of grace.—HALE IRWIN

What does it take to be a champion? Desire, dedication, determination, concentration, and the will to win.—PATTY BERG

Some people think they are concentrating when they are merely worrying.—BOBBY JONES

I guess the allure of golf is really the next shot . . . always trying to hit it perfectly, to get that feeling.—CURTIS STRANGE

I play with friends, but we don't play friendly games.
—BEN HOGAN

Don't hurry. Don't worry. You're only here on a short visit, so don't forget to stop and smell the flowers.—WALTER HAGEN

Focus on remedies, not faults.—JACK NICKLAUS

Desire is the bottom line. You've got to have 100 percent desire. Anything less is complacency.—TOM WATSON

Thinking instead of acting is the number-one golf disease.
—SAM SNEAD

I think I've been driven more by the fear of failure than the joy of success.—PAT BRADLEY

If you have to remind yourself to concentrate during competition you've got no chance to concentrate.—BOBBY NICHOLS

The mind messes up more shots than the body.—TOMMY BOLT

Golf is a difficult game, but it's a little easier if you trust your instincts. It's too hard a game to try to play like someone else.
—NANCY LOPEZ

Golf is a spiritual game. It's like Zen. You have to let your mind take over.—AMY ALCOTT

To me, the gallery becomes nothing but a wall. I don't even see faces.—Lanny Wadkins

A bad attitude is worse than a bad swing.—Payne Stewart

Of all the hazards, fear is the worst.—Sam Snead

A great round of golf is a lot like a terrible round. You drift into a zone, and it is hard to break out of it.—Al Geiberger

Trust your "muscle memory" to take over.—Ernie Els

Keep your sense of humor. There's enough stress in the rest of your life not to let bad shots ruin a game you're supposed to enjoy.—Amy Alcott

Out on the golf course factors such as wind speed, pin position, distance to the flag, and any hazards can play havoc with your decision making.—Ernie Els

Be decisive. A wrong decision is generally less disastrous than indecision.—Bernhard Langer

You can talk about strategy all you want, but what really matters is resiliency.—Hale Irwin

The zone is the ability to give 110 percent of your attention and your focus to the shot. When I'm on the tee, I'll see a divot in the fairway and try to run my ball over that divot—and succeed. That's the zone.—Nick Price

All of us have an "inner clock," a certain pace at which we function most comfortably and effectively.—KEN VENTURI

Confidence is everything. From there, it's a small step to winning.—CRAIG STADLER

Thus confidence has to be the golfer's greatest single weapon on the green.—JACK NICKLAUS

We all choke. You just try to choke last.—TOM WATSON

I'm very tightly wound. All that jabbering is a pressure valve. I couldn't do without it.—LEE TREVINO

Fear ruins more golf shots, for duffer and star, than any other one factor.—TOMMY ARMOUR

A tense mind breeds tense muscles, and tense muscles make you feel clumsy, out of gear.—JACK NICKLAUS

Putting affects the nerves more than anything else. I would actually get nauseated over three-footers, and there were tournaments when I couldn't get a meal down for four days.
—BYRON NELSON

That ball sits there and says, "Now idiot, don't hit me in the hazard. Don't hit me over there, hit me on the green. You think you can, idiot? I doubt if you can. Especially when you're choking your guts out."—DAVIS LOVE III

[Golf's] a compromise between what your ego wants you to do, what experience tells you to do, and what your nerves let you do.—BRUCE CRAMPTON

We all choke, and the man who says he doesn't choke is lying like hell.—LEE TREVINO

The person I fear most in the last two rounds is myself.
—TOM WATSON

The number-one source of pressure and choking is that you don't want to let your teammates down. It's the only time all year when you care more about others than yourself. It evokes strange responses in people. Playing for your country is big. But not wanting to let down your peers is bigger.
—JOHNNY MILLER (on the Ryder Cup)

To control your mind and body throughout a round of golf with all its pressures and frustrations is probably the single biggest challenge in golf.—GREG NORMAN

I do some form of breathing exercises during a pressure situation. It definitely helps. Every time, before I hit a key shot, I take a deep breath and cleanse the mind.—PAUL AZINGER

My butterflies are still going strong. I just hope they are flying in formation.—LARRY MIZE

Addressing a golf ball would seem to be a simple matter; that is, to the uninitiated who cannot appreciate that a golf ball can hold more terrors than a spacious auditorium packed with people.—BOBBY JONES

The pressure gets worse the older you get. The hole starts to look the size of a Bayer aspirin.—GARY PLAYER

You must always be positive, because your body can only do what your brain sees.—CHI CHI RODRIGUEZ

A long drive is good for the ego.—ARNOLD PALMER

Confidence is the key to putting.—TONY LEMA

There are times when a golfer must take this game by the scruff of the neck and give it a good, hard shake.—BILLY CASPER

The toughest thing for most people to learn in golf is to accept bad holes—and then forget about them.—GARY PLAYER

Like most professional golfers, I have a tendency to remember my poor shots a shade more vividly than the good ones. —BEN HOGAN

Even if you hit forty bad shots, you should still keep trying. The other fellow might have hit forty-one.—GARY PLAYER

The key to success on the tour—or at any level of play, for that matter—is not letting the down period get to you and make your game worse than it is. You just have to be patient and work your way out of it.—AL GEIBERGER

The game just embarrasses you until you feel inadequate and pathetic. You want to cry like a child.—CRAIG STADLER

The first thing I do after losing, regardless of whether I lost a close one because of a silly lapse or simply was snowed under by a rival running on a hot streak, is to forget it. I take a look at my calendar and start thinking about where we'll be playing next week, and I'll show 'em then!—NANCY LOPEZ

It's terrifying to think of all the gremlins that can creep into your game. Our margin for error is infinitesimal.
—ROGER MALTBIE

If you hit a bad shot, just tell yourself it is great to be alive, relaxing and walking around on a beautiful golf course. The next shot will be better. —AL GEIBERGER

When you miss a shot, never think of what you did wrong. Come up to the next shot thinking of what you must do right.
—TOMMY ARMOUR

There is nothing so demoralizing as missing a short putt.
—BOBBY JONES

You know you can't hide. It's like you're walking down the fairway naked. The gallery knows what you've done, every other player knows, and, worst of all, you know. That's when you find out if you're a competitor.—HALE IRWIN

If I ever think anybody is better than me, then I can never be the best. I always have to believe I'm the best.—PAYNE STEWART

You'll never increase your driving distance without a positive mental attitude. Confidence is vital.—GREG NORMAN

Be brave, be bold, and take your best shot.—GAY BREWER

Game Day ...

It's not whether you win or lose, but whether I win or lose.
—SANDY LYLE

The competitor inside you knows what has to be done. If the game doesn't eat you up inside, you can't possibly be a great player.—LEE TREVINO

I turn mean with a six-stroke lead. I'm not happy with a two-shot win. I want more. I want to demoralize them.
—JOHNNY MILLER

"It is not solely the capacity to make great shots that makes champions, but the essential quality of making very few bad shots.—TOMMY ARMOUR

No matter what a player does the rest of his playing days, he will be most remembered for winning major titles.
—PETER JACOBSEN

Just to play in it is great. To do well in it is fantastic. To win it is a dream.—IAN BAKER-FINCH (after winning the 1991 British Open)

This is the real World Series of Golf.
—TOM WATSON (on the British Open)

It's sort of a war out there. There's a mental discipline involved unlike at regular tour events, where the guys think they are entitled to make a birdie all the time.—HALE IRWIN (on the U.S. Open)

Winning in Scotland beats winning anywhere else. I'm a traditionalist and a sentimentalist and there's nothing like winning a championship in the birthplace of golf. This tournament is what golf is all about. You cannot love golf any more than you do when you come down the eighteenth fairway of this golf course a champion.—TOM WATSON (after winning the British Open for the third time at Muirfield in 1980)

Playing in the U.S. Open is like tippy-toeing through hell.
—JERRY MCGEE

The Masters is a perfect example of how the pressure of golf— and the buildup about how important it is—can change you so that you hardly know yourself.—JOE INMAN

I was afraid to move my lips in front of the TV cameras. The commissioner probably would have fined me just for what I was thinking.—TOM WEISKOPF (on bad shots in the 1980 Masters)

I get too jazzed up. The first round has killed me for fifteen straight years.—JOHNNY MILLER (on the Masters)

I've never been to heaven and, thinkin' back on my life, I probably won't get a chance to go. I guess the Masters is as close as I'm going to get.—FUZZY ZOELLER

When you lose a Major, it's like a death in the family.
—KEN VENTURI

Only about fifty or sixty times a day.—TOM KITE (on being asked if he still thought about losing the 1989 U.S. Open)

I didn't play my best golf, but I kept focused better than I ever had. I stayed in the present tense all week.—TOM KITE (after winning the 1992 U.S. Open)

That walk was the warmest feeling and the coldest streak down my back of my life.—FUZZY ZOELLER (about his walk up the eighteenth fairway after winning the 1984 U.S. Open)

I never exaggerate. I just remember big.—CHI CHI RODRIGUEZ

The Other Guy . . .

I loved playing with [Ben] Hogan because I knew he wouldn't say anything to me. That was good, because it helped me concentrate better.—SAM SNEAD

He [Gary Player] has milked more success out of his natural ability than any other athlete I know.—SAM SNEAD

The best sand player I have ever seen is, without doubt, Gary Player. . . . Playing against him, you begin hoping he'll be on grass rather than in sand anytime he misses a green.
—JACK NICKLAUS

He [Arnold Palmer] combined grace, force, and brute strength in an unnatural motion that seemed perfectly suited to his personality.—PETER JACOBSEN

He [Arnold Palmer] knows how to deal with people. He's probably the greatest people person in the history of golf.
—MARK O'MEARA

I used to think Arnold Palmer could walk on water. Now I know it.—CHI CHI RODRIGUEZ (after Palmer made two holes-in-one on the same hole in two days in 1986)

I think he [Jack Nicklaus] has more belief in himself, more supreme confidence, than any golfer ever. He thinks he deserves to win and that he's destined to win. So he does win. It's written all over him.—BEN CRENSHAW

[Jack] Nicklaus is able to put himself in an intense frame of mind, where nothing breaks his concentration and he can almost will the ball into the hole.—BEN CRENSHAW

One of the best I've seen at keeping his routine constant in the most critical situations is Lee Trevino. He takes the same amount of time and makes the same moves for a shot that will win him a major championship as he does in a practice round.
—AL GEIBERGER

Lee Trevino relieves his tensions by talking all the time, to other people, to himself, even sometimes in midswing. Man, how he talks!—JACK NICKLAUS

People talk about Tom Watson not having any personality, but he's one hell of a golfer. He's beating all our brains out. If it matters, he's also a nice guy.—JACK NICKLAUS

If I had to choose one player to hit a life-or-death five-foot putt, it would be Tom Watson in his prime. The guy had absolutely no fear.—PETER JACOBSEN

One of the qualities that separates guys like Seve Ballesteros and Lee Trevino from the rest of the world is an intangible—imagination.—GREG NORMAN

Greg Norman is good for golf because he plays with such bravado. He's confident and flamboyant and he hits shots that other players can't hit.—PETER JACOBSEN

Greg Norman can lead the golf tournament, throw the party that night, and entertain everybody till the wee hours, then wake up the next day and beat your brains out.—PETER JACOBSEN

To me, he's [Nick Faldo] very boring. He's never in the trees or in the water. He's not the best driver, not the best putter. He's just the best at everything.—FRED COUPLES

Of Courses . . .

When I first look at designing a hole, I consider what Mother Nature has already created on that property, and then I try to mold a golf hole that fits very naturally into what is there. . . . I guess you could say that Mother Nature is a codesigner of each of my courses.—JACK NICKLAUS

Hazards are like spices that a designer sprinkles on a course to give it flavor.—ROBERT TRENT JONES

Golf is not a fair game, so why build a course fair?
—PETER DYE

No other game combines the wonder of nature with the discipline of sport in such carefully planned ways. A great golf course both frees and challenges a golfer's mind.—TOM WATSON

Approach the golf course as a friend, not an enemy.
—ARNOLD PALMER

There is an ideal route for every golf hole ever built. The more precisely you can identify it, the greater your chances for success.—JACK NICKLAUS

I can't swing the way I want to with four sweaters and my pajamas and a rain jacket on.—LEE TREVINO (on playing in Scotland)

The Old Course is a puzzle . . . and no one's ever going to completely figure it out.—TOM WATSON (on St. Andrews)

I have already said hundreds of times that I like it better than any golf course I have ever played and although I have played it many, many times, its charm for me increases with every round.—BOBBY JONES (on St. Andrews)

The reason the Road Hole is the hardest par-4 in the world is because it's a par-5.—BEN CRENSHAW (on St. Andrews's seventeenth hole)

To me, the ground here is hallowed. The grass grows greener, the trees bloom better, there is even warmth to the rocks ... somehow or other the sun seems to shine brighter on the Country Club than any other place I have known.
—FRANCIS OUIMET

One of the scariest opening holes in golf.—TONY JACKLIN (on the first hole at Muirfield, Scotland)

The Augusta National course, where the Masters tournament is held annually, reminds me of a mouse trap with a piece of cheese in the middle. If you get too greedy the trap will crush you.—GARY PLAYER

The course is perfection and it asks perfection.—NICK FALDO (on Augusta National)

It's like a black widow. It seduces you, entices you, romances you—and then it stings you, kills you emotionally.
—MAC O'GRADY (on Augusta National)

If there's a golf course in heaven, I hope it's like Augusta National. I just don't want an early tee time.—GARY PLAYER

Ask every professional on tour what his five favorite golf courses are in the world, and the one name that will be on everybody's list is Pebble Beach.—TOM WATSON

If I had only one more round of golf to play, I would choose to play it at Pebble Beach.—JACK NICKLAUS

If you're five over when you hit this tee, it's the best place in the world to commit suicide.—LEE TREVINO (on Pebble Beach's sixth hole)

Gurus ...

Don't be too proud to take lessons. I'm not.—JACK NICKLAUS

No one becomes a champion without help.—JOHNNY MILLER

The practice ground is an evil place. It's full of so-called coaches waiting to pounce. You can see them waiting to dish their mumbo-jumbo. To hell with coaches.—ERNIE ELS

I've never had a coach in my life. When I find one who can beat me, then I'll listen.—LEE TREVINO

Rhythm and timing we all must have, yet no one knows how to teach either.—BOBBY JONES

Seniors ...

You're never too old to play golf. If you can walk, you can play.—LOUISE SUGGS

Retire to what? I'm a golfer and a fisherman. I've got no place to retire to.—JULIUS BOROS

Why should I play against those flat bellies when I can play against these round bellies?—LEE TREVINO (on why he joined the Senior Tour)

Tom Watson (*Layne Murdoch*)

Reporters used to ask me questions about the condition of my game. Now all they want to know is about the condition of my health.—Jack Nicklaus

His nerve, his memory, and I can't remember the third thing.
—Lee Trevino (on being asked what three things an aging golfer loses)

You know this is the Senior Tour when your back goes out more than you do.—Bob Bruce

They keep talking about the Big Four—Palmer, Nicklaus, Player, and Trevino. I just want to be the fifth wheel in case somebody gets a flat.—Chi Chi Rodriguez (on the Senior Tour)

When you get up there in years, the fairways get longer and the holes get smaller.—Bobby Locke

That's the easiest 69 I ever made.—Walter Hagen (about his birthday)

Golf and the Fair Sex . . .

I think it's both thrilling and wonderful to be female, both in being a woman and in being a woman golfer.—Nancy Lopez

When we complain about conditions, we're just bitches. But when the men complain, people think, Well, it really must be hard.—Betsy King

Because women are not as strong as men, it's even more important for them to be fundamentally correct in form than it is for men.—Kathy Whitworth

I'll take a two-shot penalty, but I'll be damned if I'm going to play the ball where it lies.—ELAINE JOHNSON (after her ball bounced off a tree into her bra)

I just hitch up my girdle and let 'er fly.—BABE DIDRIKSON ZAHARIAS (on the secret of her driving distance)

If I didn't have to worry about these things, I could really hit it a mile.—BABE DIDRIKSON ZAHARIAS (after adjusting her bra)

Well, that lot's full. Let's see if I can park this baby someplace else.—JoANNE CARNER (on hitting two drives in a row into a parking lot)

Cads and Caddies . . .

We work as a team—I hand him the clubs and he makes the shots.—NATHANIEL "IRONMAN" AVERY (Arnold Palmer's caddie)

If I needed advice from my caddie, he'd be hitting the shots and I'd be carrying the bag.—BOBBY JONES

Caddies are a breed of their own. If you shoot a 66, they say, "Man, we shot 66!" But go out and shoot 77, and they say, "Hell, he shot 77!"—LEE TREVINO

Nobody but you and your caddie cares what you do out there, and if your caddie is betting against you, he doesn't care either. —LEE TREVINO

Every golfer has his own quirks, and it's the caddie's job to adapt to them.—PETER JACOBSEN

If each time a player and a caddie split up was actually a divorce, most tour players would have been 'married' more times than Zsa Zsa and Liz combined.—Peter Jacobsen

The Proper Tools: Equipment and Clothing . . .

Perhaps the most important thing I can tell you about equipment is to experiment and keep an open mind.—Gary Player

I know you can get fined for throwing a club. What I want to know is if you can get fined for throwing a caddie.—Tommy Bolt

Properly fitted clubs are the only part of improved golf that anyone can buy.—Tommy Armour

The most exquisitely satisfying act in the world of golf is that of throwing a club. The full backswing, the delayed wrist action, the flowing follow-through, followed by that unique whirring sound, reminiscent only of a flock of passing starlings, is without parallel in the sport.—Henry Longhurst (writer)

To be a true artist on the greens, you should be as selective in choosing a putter as, say, a master violinist would be in choosing his or her instrument.—Paul Runyan

No game is as exacting as golf in that so many specifications must be met to make a precision fit of implement and player. —Tommy Armour

It's so important to have a putter you feel confident you can hole putts with. It takes pressure off your whole game and you can just relax and play your best.—Greg Kraft

Those are the times when you look down and stare at your club—as if, for some reason, it was your club's fault instead of your own pathetic swing.—MARK O'MEARA (on driving the ball into the water at the U.S. Open)

It's a marriage. If I had to choose between my wife and my putter, I'd miss her.—GARY PLAYER

You can't let a putter think it's indispensable. I keep another one—named Number Two—in the car trunk. I switch at least once a year, just to prove to Betsy she can be switched.
—FUZZY ZOELLER

Knickers are good for my golf game. They're cooler in hot weather because the air circulates in them and they're warmer in cold weather because they trap the body heat.—PAYNE STEWART

I even enjoy the mingled pleasure and discomfort of breaking in a new pair of golf shoes.—ARNOLD PALMER

I just might open a school for club-throwers, so players could get their clubs going in the right direction and at the right angle so that the club doesn't get damaged.—TOMMY BOLT

Eye of the Tiger . . .

When you are ahead, don't take it easy, kill them. After the finish, then be a sportsman.—EARL WOODS (to his son Tiger Woods)

I thought it was a new golf course.—SANDY LYLE (on being asked what he thought of an up-and-coming amateur named Tiger Woods)

To look out here and see so many kids, I think that's wonderful. They see someone they can relate to, me being so young.
—TIGER WOODS

It's just one of those days when you hit what I would consider perfect putts. I hit edge after edge after edge.—TIGER WOODS

I hate to lose. But in golf, everybody loses, because it is so hard mentally.—TIGER WOODS

I don't think we've had a whole lot happen in what, ten years? I mean, some guys here have come on and won a few tournaments, but nobody has sustained and dominated. I think we might have somebody now.—JACK NICKLAUS (on Tiger Woods)

It's really nice seeing more minorities in the gallery. I think that's where the game should go and will go.—TIGER WOODS

I'm here to play golf. Granted I don't get sunburned as easily as you guys, but that's about it. As far as anything else, I'm just like anybody else. I'm trying to get the ball in the hole in as few shots as I can.—TIGER WOODS (at the 1997 Masters)

12

Best and Worst: The Good, the Bad, and the Dangerous in the Game of Golf

These are the hazards of golf: the unpredictability of your own body chemistry, the rub of the green on the courses, the wind and the weather, the bee that lands on your ball or on the back of your neck while you are putting, the sudden noise while you are swinging, the whole problem of playing the game at high mental tension and low physical tension.

—ARNOLD PALMER

The Twelve Best Things About Golf

1. It's a game of great concentration and control.
2. The variables are enormous: golf course, equipment, wind and other elements (nature as both friend and foe), partnering.

3. You get to commune with nature.
4. You get to wear unorthodox clothing.
5. The balls are inexpensive.
6. You get to hold a phallic extension.
7. You get to tell your wife it's Zen-like.
8. You get to ride around in a motorized cart.
9. When you get too old, there's always the Senior Tour.
10. You get to kill insects.
11. Golf is good for business networking.
12. You can be out of shape and still play the game.

Three ways golf is different from baseball:
1. In golf the ball doesn't move until you hit it.
2. In golf, when you hit a foul ball, you have to play it.
3. Baseball is a game of inches; golf is a game of millimeters.

The Twelve Worst Things About Golf

1. Blind dumb luck is a significant factor in the game's outcome.
2. The game moves at a snail's pace.
3. Memorizing the sum total of official golf rules is next to impossible.
4. Golf results are always listed after other sports.
5. Professional golf is an "inner circle" game without the broad base of interest that baseball, basketball, and football have.
6. The great accessibility of amateur golf to average people throws its "sports legitimacy" into question—everybody and his brother's a golfer!

7. The subject of golf makes for boring feature films.
8. Golf tans are uneven.
9. Games are not called because of rain.
10. Golf is used as a ploy for business networking.
11. Insects get to bite you.
12. You can play the game and still be out of shape.

The Tour is not what most people seem to think. It's not all sunshine and pretty girls and cheering crowds. It's life without roots. It's a potentially rewarding life, but also a frustrating life. There's no real opponent except your own stupid mental and physical mistakes.—FRANK BEARD

Ten Golf Dangers

1. Lightning—Avoid open areas, elevated areas, isolated trees, bodies of water, metal objects (such as golf carts); take refuge in lightning shelters and buildings, such as the clubhouse or maintenance facilities, or in automobiles.
2. Heat stroke—Drink plenty of fluids.
3. Sunburn—If you're a regular, wear sunblock; don't underestimate melanoma.
4. Flying golf balls—They can create skull indentations. When you hear "fore," duck and cover your head.
5. Golf clubs—Stand clear of backswings and watch out for flying clubs when someone has a temper tantrum.
6. Reckless golf cart drivers—There's no ticketing for drunk driving on golf courses. And when you're driving, watch where you're going and stick to level ground.

Sam Snead

7. Water hazards—Don't fall in bodies of water.
8. Chemicals—Golf courses use toxic pesticides and herbicides. Don't be cleaning the ball with your tongue or licking your fingers, and don't play barefoot. After a round, wash your hands.
9. Poisonous plants—Poison ivy and poison oak are all too widespread.
10. Creatures—Bees, hornets, wasps, yellow jackets, spiders, scorpions, snakes (rattlesnakes, water moccasins, copperheads, and coral snakes are all poisonous), racoons (can be rabid), squirrels (so can squirrels), and, in the Southeast, alligators are all a possibility.

Four Ways to Make Other Golfers Dangerous

1. Playing the wrong ball—You could get bushwacked.
2. Fudging your golf score—People have been executed for less.
3. Speaking while someone is putting—This can lead to ball-in-mouth disease.
4. Laughing at someone else's mistake—Let us not forget the derivation of the term *club*.

A spectator's note: Cursing in the gallery can get you deported—that privilege is reserved for the golfers.

13

Organizations and Tournaments

*It's like the America's Cup. I never even heard of
it until we lost it.*

—RAYMOND FLOYD
(on the Ryder Cup)

Golf is well organized, there's no question about that. The following are the most important organizations and tournaments.

Important Organizations

Ladies Professional Golfing Association (LPGA)   Offices in
Daytona Beach, Florida. Founded in 1950; certifies women
professionals.

Professional Golfers Association (PGA)   Offices in Palm Beach
Gardens, Florida. Founded in 1916; certifies golf pros. It has
about nine thousand members, most of them golf club or
resort instructors. Several hundred pros tour the country
playing on the PGA Tour—as supervised by the Tournament
Players Division. Since 1980, the PGA has also run the PGA
Senior Tour. In 1940 the PGA Hall of Fame was founded to

honor golfers who through their lifetime playing ability have made outstanding contributions to the game.

Royal and Ancient Golf Club of St. Andrews (R&A) Offices in St. Andrews, Scotland. Founded in 1754; framed original golf code; along with the United States Golf Association, revises the Rules of Golf every four years. It runs the British Open and British Amateur championship.

United States Golf Association (USGA) Offices in Far Hills, New Jersey. Founded in 1894 with five clubs; now more than six thousand clubs; along with the R&A, provides standards and sets rules; conducts U.S. Open and Amateur and Women's Open and Amateur; sponsors Walker Cup, Curtis Cup, and Americas Cup.

Important Tournaments

British Amateur Annual tournament for amateurs; held at different sites; inaugurated in 1885.

British Open Annual tournament for amateurs and professionals (one of the Majors); held at different courses in July; inaugurated in 1860.

Curtis Cup An annual team tournament for women amateurs, Great Britain versus the United States; biennial at different courses; inaugurated in 1922.

Du Maurier Ltd. Classic An annual tournament for women amateurs and pros (a Major); held at the Edmonton Country Club, Edmonton, Alberta, Canada, in August; inaugurated in 1973.

Eisenhower Trophy (Men's World Amateur Team Championship): An international team tournament for amateurs; biennial at different courses; inaugurated in 1958.

Espiritu Santo Trophy (Women's World Amateur Team Championship): An international team tournament for women amateurs; biennial at different courses; inaugurated in 1964.

Masters An annual invitational tournament for professionals (one of the Majors); held in April at Augusta National; inaugurated in 1934.

Nabisco Dinah Shore An annual tournament for women amateurs and professionals (one of the women's Majors); held at Mission Hills Country Club, Rancho Mirage, California, in March; inaugurated in 1973.

PGA Championship A tournament for pros (one of the Majors); held in August at different courses; inaugurated in 1916.

Ryder Cup A tournament for professionals (originally Great Britain versus the United States until the British team became part of the European team in 1979); biennial at different courses; inaugurated in 1927.

Shun Nomura Trophy (World Senior Amateur Team Championship): An international team tournament for Senior professionals; biennial; at different courses; inaugurated in 1967.

U.S. Amateur A men's tournament for amateurs; held at different courses in August; inaugurated in 1895.

U.S. Open A men's tournament for amateurs and pros (a Major); held in June on different courses; inaugurated in 1895.

U.S. Senior Open A tournament for amateurs and professionals for men over fifty years of age; held on different courses in July; inaugurated in 1980.

U.S. Women's Amateur A tournament for women amateurs; held at different courses in August; inaugurated in 1895.

The seventh hole at Pebble Beach (*Pebble Beach Company*)

U.S. Women's Open   A tournament for women amateurs and professionals; held at different courses in late May or early June; inaugurated in 1946.

Walker Cup   A team tournament for amateurs; Great Britain versus the United States; biennial at different courses; inaugurated in 1922.

World Cup   An international tournament for two-man teams of professionals (an International Trophy is also given to the individual with the lowest score); held at different courses; inaugurated as the Canada Cup in 1953 (became the World Cup in 1967).

World Series of Golf   A tournament for the winners of the four Majors in a thirty-six-hole contest; held at Firestone in Ohio; inaugurated in 1962.

Other Golf Awards

LPGA Player-of-the-Year Award   Awarded to the woman golfer on the U.S. Tour with the most consistent and outstanding record; inaugurated in 1966.

PGA Player-of-the-Year Award   Awarded to the golfer on the U.S. Tour with the most consistent and outstanding record; based on scoring average, money winnings, Vardon Trophy, Ryder Cup points, etc.; inaugurated in 1948.

Vardon Trophy   Awarded to the golfer maintaining the lowest scoring average in PGA events.

Vare Trophy   Awarded to the woman golfer maintaining the lowest scoring average in LPGA events.

14

Golf Books, Publications, and Moving Images

The smaller the ball used in the sport, the better the book.

—GEORGE PLIMPTON
(writer)

[Golf's] best medium is not television, radio, or the eye. Even more than baseball, it's the sport of words.

—THOMAS BOSWELL
(writer)

Don't stop here. Keep going. After all, if you're not playing golf, what else could be better than to read about it, or, if you must, watch a video about it? Golf has been blessed with wonderful writing—enjoy!

Helpful Introductory Books on Golf

Golf, by Bernard Gallacher and Mark Wilson ("The Teach Yourself Series," NTC, 1991).

Golf for Beginners: The Official Survival Guide, by Scott J. Lotts and Vicki Barnes-Rothmeier (Mulligan's, 1994).

Golf for Dummies, by Gary McCord (IDG, 1996).

The Golf Handbook: The Complete Guide to the Greatest Game, by Vivien Saunders (Crown, 1997).

Golfers on Golf, by Downs MacRury (General Publishing Group, 1997).

Books on the Rules of Golf

Golf Rules: A Player's Guide, by Steve Newell (Blandford, 1995).

The New Rules of Golf, by Tom Watson and Frank Hannigan (Random House, 1984).

1997 Official Rules of Golf: As Approved by the United States Golf Association and the Royal and Ancient Golf Club of St. Andrews, Scotland (Triumph, 1996).

The PGA Manual of Golf, by Gary Wiren (Macmillan, 1991).

Rules of Golf Applied, by Cliff Schrock (Masters, 1995).

Instructional Books

Advanced Golf, by Greg Norman (Charles E. Tuttle, 1995).

Ben Hogan's Power Golf, by Ben Hogan (Pocket Books, 1948).

Bobby Jones on Golf, by Robert Tyre Jones (Doubleday, 1966).

Five Lessons: The Modern Fundamentals of Golf, by Ben Hogan with Herbert Warren Wind (Simon & Schuster, 1957).

For All Who Love the Game: Lessons and Teachings for Women, by Harvey Penick (Simon & Schuster, 1995).

The Four Cornerstones of Winning Golf, by Claude "Butch" Harmon Jr. and John Andrisini (Simon & Schuster, 1996).

The Game of a Lifetime: More Lessons and Teachings, by Harvey Penick (Simon & Schuster, 1996).

Gary Player's Golf Secrets, by Gary Player (Prentice-Hall, 1962).

Getting Up and Down, by Tom Watson with Nick Seitz (Random House, 1983).

Golf for Women, by Kathy Whitlock (St. Martin's, 1990).

Golf My Way, by Jack Nicklaus with Ken Bowden (Simon & Schuster, 1974).

Golf Shotmaking With Billy Casper, by Billy Casper (Golf Digest, 1966).

Golf: The Winning Formula, by Nick Faldo with Vivien Saunders (Lyons & Burford, 1989).

Harvey Penick's Little Red Book: Lessons and Teachings for a Lifetime in Golf, by Harvey Penick (Simon & Schuster, 1992).

How to Play Golf and Professional Tips on Improving Your Score, by Sam Snead (Hall, 1952).

How to Play Your Best Golf All the Time, by Tommy Armour (Simon & Schuster, 1953).

Lessons From the Golf Greats, by David Leadbetter (HarperCollins, 1995).

My Game and Yours, by Arnold Palmer (Simon & Schuster, 1983).

Natural Golf, by John Duncan Dunn (Putnam's, 1931).

On Learning Golf, by Percy Boomer (Knopf, 1992).

Tempo: Golf's Master Key, by Al Geiberger with Larry Dennis (Golf Digest, 1980).

Trouble-Shooting, by Seve Ballesteros with Robert Green (Broadway, 1996).

The Venturi System, With Special Material on Shotmaking for the Advanced Golfer, by Ken Venturi with Al Barkow (Atheneum, 1985).

A Woman's Golf Game: Techniques and Tips From Pro Golfers, by Shirli Kaskie (Contemporary, 1982).

A Woman's Guide to Better Golf, by Judy Rankin (Contemporary, 1995).

Books on Inner Golf

Beyond the Fairway: Zen Lessons, Insights, and Inner Attitudes of Golf, by Jeff Wallach (Bantam, 1995).

Extraordinary Golf: The Art of the Possible, by Fred Shoemaker (Perigee, 1996).

Golf Is Not a Game of Perfect, by Dr. Bob Rotella with Bob Cullen (Simon & Schuster, 1995).

The Mental Game of Golf: A Guide to Peak Performance, by Patrick J. Cohn (Diamond, 1994).

A wonderfully philosophical book on golf is Arnold Haultain's *The Mystery of Golf: A Brief Account of Its Origin, Antiquity and Romance; Its Uniqueness; Its Curiousness; and Its Difficulty; Its Anatomical, Philosophical, and Moral Properties; Together With Diverse Concepts on Other Matters to It Appertaining* (published by Houghton Mifflin in 1908 and reissued by Applewood in 1995). You'll find gems like: "Golf is the most jealous of mistresses"; and "There are three things as unfathomable as they are fascinating to the masculine mind: metaphysics, golf, and the feminine heart"; and "Golf, in short, is not so much a game as it is a creed and a religion."

A Book About Equipment

The Insider's Guide to Golf Equipment: The Fully Illustrated Comprehensive Directory of Brand-Name Clubs and Accessories, by Nick Mastroni (Perigee, 1997).

Books About the History of Golf

Fifty Years of American Golf, by H. B. Martin (Dodd, Mead, 1936).

Golf: A Woman's History, by Elinor Nickerson (McFarland, 1986).

Golf: The History of an Obsession, by David Stirk (Phaidon, 1987).

The Golf Immortals, by Tom Scott and Geoffrey Cousins (Hart, 1969).

Golf Legends, by Greg Garber (Freidman/Fairfax, 1994).

Golf Magazine's Encyclopedia of Golf, edited by John M. Ross (Harper, 1979).

The Historical Dictionary of Golfing Terms: From 1500 to the Present, by Peter Davies (Michael Kesend, 1992).

The Rules of the Green: A History of the Rules of Golf, by Kenneth G. Chapman (Triumph, 1997).

The Unplayable Lie: The Untold Story of Women and Discrimination in American Golf, by Marcia Chambers (Golf Digest, 1995).

The World of Golf, by Charles Price (Random House, 1962).

Books With Golf Anecdotes

"And Then Jack Said to Arnie . . .": A Collection of the Greatest True Golf Stories of All Time, by Don Wade (Contemporary, 1992).

The Book of Golf Disasters, by Peter Dobereiner (Harper-Perennial, 1983).

The Golf Hall of Shame, by Bruce Nash and Allan Zullo (Pocket Books, 1989).

The Golf Nut's Book of Amazing Feats and Records, by Bruce Nash and Allan Zullo with George White (Contemporary, 1994).

Perfect Lies: A Century of Great Golf Stories, edited by William Hallberg (Fireside, 1989).

Books About Golf Courses

The American Golfer's Guide: Over 500 of the Best American Golf Courses Open to the Public, by Hubert Pedroli and Mary Tiegreen (Turner, 1992).

The Anatomy of a Golf Course: The Art of Golf Architecture, by Tom Doak (Lyons & Burford, 1992).

Bury Me in a Pot Bunker: Golf Through the Eyes of the Game's Most Challenging Course Designer, by Pete Dye with Mark Shaw (Addison-Wesley, 1995).

The Course Beautiful, by A. W. Tillinghast (Treewolf, 1995).

Golf by Design, by Robert Trent Jones Jr. (Little, Brown, 1993).

The Golf Course, by Geoffrey S. Cornish and Ronald E. Whitten (W. H. Smith, 1981).

Golf Courses of the U.S. Open, by John Steinbreder (Taylor Publishing, 1996)

Golf Digest's 4,200 Best Places to Play, (Fodor's/Golf Digest, 1995).

Golf Resorts of the World: The Best Places to Stay and Play, by Brian McCallen (Harry N. Abrams, 1993).

Buried Lies: True Tales and Tall Stories From the PGA Tour, by Peter Jacobsen with Jack Sheehan (G. P Putnam's Sons, 1993).

Down the Fairway: The Golf Life and Play of Robert T. Jones, by Robert T. Jones Jr., and O. B. Keeler (Minton, Balch, 1927).

The Education of a Golfer, by Sam Snead with Al Stump (Simon & Schuster, 1962).

The Education of a Woman Golfer, by Nancy Lopez with Peter Schwed (Simon & Schuster, 1979).

Hogan, by Curt Sampson (Rutledge Hill Press, 1996)

Jack Nicklaus: My Story, by Jack Nicklaus with Ken Bowden (Simon & Schuster, 1997).

John Daly: Wild Thing, by William Wartman (Harper, 1996).

The Little Black Book, by Byron Nelson (Summit, 1995).

My Partner, Ben Hogan, by Jimmy Demaret (McGraw-Hill, 1954).

The Snake in the Sandtrap (and Other Misadventures on the Golf Tour), by Lee Trevino and Sam Blair (Owl, 1985).

Thirty Years of Championship Golf, by Gene Sarazen (Prentice-Hall, 1950).

This Life I've Led, by Babe Didrikson Zaharias (A. S. Barnes, 1955).

Tiger Woods: The Making of a Champion, by Tim Rosaforte (St. Martin's, 1997).

Training a Tiger: A Father's Guide to Raising a Winner in Both Golf and Life, by Earl Woods with Pete McDaniel (Harper-Collins, 1997).

The Walter Hagen Story, by Walter Hagen with Margaret Seaton Heck (Simon & Schuster, 1956).

Books by Hackers

Divots, Shanks, Gimmes, Mulligans, and Chili Dips: A Life in 18 Holes, by Glen Waggoner (Villard, 1993).

Fairways and Greens: The Best Golf Writing of Dan Jenkins, by Dan Jenkins (Doubleday, 1994).

Golf Dreams, by John Updike (Alfred A. Knopf, 1997).

Golf in the Kingdom, by Michael Murphy (Penguin, 1994).

Strokes of Genius, by Thomas Boswell (Penguin, 1987).

Golf Publications

These publications, sold at magazine stores and newstands, and available at your local library, offer tips on your game and can help you stay up-to-date on tournament results, golfing vacations, new golf equipment, etc.:

Golf Digest—monthly
The Golfer—biannual
Golf Illustrated—monthly
Golf Magazine—monthly
Golf Monthly—monthly
Golf Tips—nine issues a year
Golf for Women—six issues a year
Golf World—forty-six issues a year
Golf World International—monthly (British)
Links: The Best of Golf—seven issues a year
Play Better Golf—annual
Senior Golfer—ten issues a year

Instructional Videos

Instructional videos are helpful in understanding the mechanics of golf—seeing a swing is very different from reading about it (a good way to order a video is through ads in the magazines listed above):

The Art of Putting—Ben Crenshaw
Beginning Golf for Women—Donna White
Couples on Tempo—Fred Couples
Golf's Greatest Moments: 100 Years of American Golf
Golf My Way: Jack Nicklaus
   Volume 1: *Hitting the Shots*
   Volume 2: *Playing the Games*
Harvey Penick's Little Red Video (and *The Little Green Video*)
Leadbetter's Simple Secrets—David Leadbetter (also *The Full Golf Swing and Faults and Fixes*)
Nick Faldo's Tips and Drills

Golf Online

Are you wired? If so, you will want to explore the golf universe at your desk with the click of the mouse. Golf-related websites number in the thousands now. A good one to start with is:

The Golf Net (www.sdgolf.com): A listing of golf-related sites on the Internet. You choose where you want to go.

Then you might want to check out:

Golf (www.golf.com): NBC and *Golf Digest* both provide data for this site.
Golf USA (www.southeast.org/golfusa): A good starting point if you're shopping for golf-related products with discount pricing.
GolfWeb: Everything Golf on the World Wide Web! (www.golfweb.com): As the subtitle says, this website keeps

you up-to-date on all aspects of the game: tournament results, course information, and a pro shop for buying equipment (plus a bulletin board for used equipment).

The 19th Hole (www.golfball.com): This website has the feel of a real clubhouse. You can make your presence and opinions known.

PGA Tour (www.PGA.com): Keep up-to-date on the Tour and lots of other golf info.

World Golf (www.worldgolf.com): If you're planning an international golf-related vacation, this is a great way to do it.

You'll also find that individual golf courses have their own home pages, as do equipment manufacturers.

For this left-handed author, perhaps the most important site of all is www.dca.net/golf/index.html. Yes, this is the official website of the National Association of Left-Handed Golfers, whose credo is (or ought to be): You're not on the wrong side of the ball. Doubtless, prominent lefties Pete Mickelson, Bob Charles, and Russ Cochran will be cyber-highlighted.

Golf Video Games

The following are three of the best computer golf games, available in computer software stores (and they're more than just games now; as electronic simulators, they help you think golf):

Links386 (Access Software)
Microsoft Golf (Microsoft and Access Software)
PGA Tour '96 (Electronic Arts)

15

Golf Trivia? Not!

They say golf is like life but don't believe them.
Golf is more complicated than that.

—GARDNER DICKINSON

You've taken the golf quiz on information every golf devotee should know. You've learned a lot about golf in the ensuing chapters. Here are some more golf factoids. Since it's golf, I refuse to call it trivia. It's history! It's sociology! It's physics! It's the game of life!

Five Golf Movies Not to Miss

Caddyshack (1980)   Rodney Dangerfield is hilarious in this silly, raunchy, over-the-top comedy about a bore who invades a staid country club. Chevy Chase, Bill Murray, Brian Doyle-Murray, and Ted Knight provide further delicious nonsense.

Dead Solid Perfect (1988)   Taken from the Dan Jenkins novel, Randy Quaid (a seriously good golfer) plays a struggling young pro on the tour, and Kathryn Harrold plays his long-suffering wife. Funny, true, and even occasionally poignant.

Payne Stewart (*Layne Murdoch*)

Happy Gilmore (1996)   Couldn't be any dumber, but who cares? Adam Sandler is amusingly absurd in this story of a hockey fanatic who discovers that he's a gifted (if utterly unorthodox) golfing natural.

Pat and Mike (1952)   The class act in my fivesome, this George Cukor-directed film has small-time sports promoter Spencer Tracy guiding the career of the sophisticated, gifted, and slightly fragile Katharine Hepburn as she attempts to conquer the woman's game. Hepburn looks very comfortable swinging a club, and this light but flavorsome flick delivers ample Tracy-Hepburn juice.

Tin Cup (1996)   Kevin Costner, another actor who's links legit, plays a down-and-completely-out pro who gets one more chance at the brass ring.

Bonus Choice

The Golf Specialist (1930)   An eighteen-minute, black-and-white short featuring W. C. Fields—who could really play our favorite game—reprising an old vaudeville sketch in brilliant, uproarious fashion. Don't miss it.

Fun Factoids

Before 1764, golf courses had twenty-two holes. In 1764, the Royal and Ancient Golf Club combined eight of them into four, making the number eighteen.

For almost sixty years, different-size golf balls were used in Great Britain and the United States. All balls used to be 1.62 inches in diameter, but in 1931 the USGA approved a 1.68-inch-diameter ball. The R & A did not change its official ball size to 1.68 inches until 1990.

The odds of making a hole-in-one are calculated to be 8,606 to 1. Go for it.

Double eagles are rarer than holes-in-one. The reason: Aces usually are made on short, par-3 holes. Double eagles are made on par-5 holes, requiring two long and accurate shots, not just one.

Golf bags were first introduced around 1870. Before that, caddies carried players' clubs in a bundle under their arm.

Iron Byron is the USGA's "robot" for testing golf balls and clubs because Byron Nelson's classic swing was used in designing it.

Byron Nelson was sometimes referred to as Lord Nelson.

A "Stimpmeter" is a device—a grooved bar—used to measure the speed of greens. A ball is placed on the bar; the bar is lifted; and the distance the ball rolls is measured. The procedure is repeated several times, and an average taken of the results.

The Jinja Golf Course in Uganda has at least two rules not usually encountered elsewhere:

1. A golf ball may be lifted from the footprint of a hippopotamus and dropped without penalty.
2. If a ball comes to rest in dangerous proximity to a crocodile, another ball may be dropped.

Walter Hagen was sometimes referred to as the Haig and Sir Walter.

The term *championship course* refers to a course requiring distance, accuracy, finesse shots, and strong putting to achieve par. An *executive course* is smaller and is so-named because executives can fit in games and still work once in a while.

According to the National Golf Foundation, 67 percent of business executives play golf.

The world's longest course is the International Golf Club in Bolton, Massachusetts—a 3,325-yard par-77. The course also boasts what is probably the world's largest green on the fifth hole—28,000 square feet.

JoAnne Carner is affectionately known on the Women's Tour as Big Mama.

The 1945 British horror film *Dead of Night* has a golf sequence.

Calamity Jane was the name of Bobby Jones's putter.

The members of the St. Andrews Club of Yonkers were called the Apple Tree Gang.

Lee Trevino's father was a professional grave digger.

Tommy Armour lost the sight in one eye while serving in the Tank Corps in World War I . . . before he turned professional and won the U.S. Open, PGA Championship, and British Open.

Many golf courses in Florida use Bermuda grass, better-suited to the climate than bent grass or *Poa annua*. Because of its coarseness, balls sit up well on it.

The Canadian Open is known as the Fifth Major.

Because there are so few golf courses in Japan, many Japanese play golf only at driving ranges.

Most courses in Japan have two greens per hole, because of climate extremes—one with bent grass, regrown each year since it burns out in the hot and humid summers, and the other with *korai*, a tougher grass imported from Korea.

Croquet-style putting—i.e., straddling the ball and hitting it as in a croquet shot—is forbidden in the Rules of Golf. Sam Snead used to putt this way.

Bobby Jones played as an amateur his entire career.

Jimmy Demaret was a nightclub singer as well as a golfer.

A common expression of the pros when they hit the ball well on a given day is "I hit it like Hogan" in reference and deference to the great Ben Hogan.

Australian David Graham was known as a designer of clubs as well as a professional golfer.

A "Cayman" course refers to a small course of about 4,000 yards in length, like the one built in the early 1980s in the Cayman Islands because of lack of land. Special balls are used. They are made to travel less distance when hit.

Tony Lema was known as Champagne Tony Lema because he promised to serve up champagne to journalists if he won the 1962 Orange County, California, Open, which he did.

South African Bobby Locke's real name is Arthur D'Arcy Locke.

Taiwanese Liang-Huan Lu is known simply as Mr. Lu.

Cary Middlecoff was called the Doc by other golfers because he was trained as a dentist.

Christy O'Connor was sometimes called Himself.

Craig Stadler is called the Walrus because of his bulk and mustache.

Joe Flynn holds the record for the lowest score for eighteen holes by throwing a golf ball—82. In 1975, on the Port Royal Course in Bermuda, he accomplished the feat at age twenty-one.

Golf balls have low ID numbers—typically 1 through 4—for no other reason than that touring pros tended to favor them out of superstition. The manufacturers simply gave up on the higher numbers.

More than 90 percent of pro golfers are married.

The mean age for PGA Tour golfers is thirty-five.

The state where most pro golfers were born is California; the state where most live is Florida.

In 1988 there were sixteen sudden-death play-offs in the forty-six PGA tournaments, setting a record.

The USGA-recommended height of a flagstick is a minimum of seven feet.

Steel shafts for golf clubs were legalized by the USGA in 1924.

The Tuctu Golf Club in Morococha, Peru, boasts the highest golf course in the world—14,335 feet above sea level.

But why is there no golf in Tibet?
1. On the Tibetan Plateau, the wind factor could send a ball a thousand miles out of bounds.
2. Trying to find a white golf ball in the white snow could delay a game up to four centuries.
